FORMULA FOR MURDER

The I.C.I. Mystery

by

R.M.BEVAN

FORMULA FOR MURDER

The I.C.I. Mystery

by

R.M.BEVAN

C.C. Publishing, Chester
(Cheshire Country Publishing)
ISBN 0 949001 21 X

First published in the United Kingdom in 2003
by Cheshire Country Publishing

A catalogue record of this book is
available from the British Library.

CONTENTS

FOREWORD

Formula for Murder is a study into a double tragedy that occurred almost eighty years ago. It reopens the case into the deaths of industrialist Roscoe Brunner and his authoress wife Ethel and explores their role in events leading to the formation of Imperial Chemical Industries (I.C.I.) which came to be one of the largest companies in the world, a colossus of the 20th century.

Many books have chronicled the technical and business aspects of I.C.I., but not a single writer has ever considered the terrible personal tragedy at the heart of those frenetic first days, set as they were against a backdrop of one of the most turbulent periods in British history. Conceived over a cup of American coffee and put together inside twelve incredible weeks during the closing months of 1926, the creation of I.C.I. involved a merger of four companies with 70,000 workers and more than £65 million of assets. It came to be a testimony to the single-minded determination and business vision of two men, Sir Alfred Mond and Sir Harry McGowan.

That the Brunner case has escaped the detailed attention of scholarly historians is not surprising. To these it held no consequence and therefore warranted nothing more than a passing footnote. To me, however, it has held a fascination and as I followed the saga through newspapers and records, I could never relinquish the thought that there was something else, that the Brunners did not die as conveniently as history, or the company, would have us believe.

At first it may have been intuition, but the more I delved, the more convinced I became that something was wrong, that powerful forces, adept at the difficult art of scandal-burying, had succeeded in suppressing the truth by manipulating and exploiting a woefully inept police investigation and a sham of an inquest. What I also discovered, in no small measure, was a catalogue of happenings which, to this day, have never been satisfactorily explained.

How did the official Brunner file, relating to what was ostensibly a simple domestic tragedy, come to be classified with Royal and State archives, locked away under Britain's 'Hundred Years Rule' until 2026? What was the secret that the Brunners took to their grave and who was prepared to go to any lengths to protect the fragile foundations of I.C.I.?

I have not set out to deliberately demonize Sir Alfred Mond, rather to present an alternative picture of a man who was a political and industrial heavyweight of his time. He sought recognition and he possessed the wealth, but power was what he craved, supreme power. He was not driven by money, or ideals, and this book deals with one aspect in his life. It is for readers to judge for themselves.

Formula for Murder is about a tragic conflict of loyalty, big business, ambition, power, politics, treachery and murder. It is also a story about Victorian entrepreneurism and an almost rags-to-riches rise of two families, from humble beginnings to the heart of government and marriage into the Royal families of Europe. Most of all, it is about a compelling mystery that is supposed never to have existed.

R.M.Bevan

v

Ethel Brunner, Roscoe Brunner (left)
and Sir Alfred Mond.

CHAPTER ONE
THE ROEHAMPTON TRAGEDY

The chimes of Big Ben marked the half hour as the man stepped out into the London fog. 'Good night, sir,' called the doorman of the Bath Club. Roscoe Brunner did not reply; he was too preoccupied with his own thoughts and, for once, his natural easy-going politeness deserted him. In Dover Street, he purchased the evening's final edition of the London Standard which screamed with headlines concerning the prolonged national coal stoppage. Now in its eleventh month, 1926 was destined to become one of those milestone years which for ever live on in British memory. Like 1901 and the death of Queen Victoria, the outbreak of war in 1914, and the peace celebrations of 1918, this had been another year which few would ever forget as the ceaseless months of strife and the bitter conflict of the General Strike had brought Britain closer to anarchy than at any time since the Civil War.

Himself a leading industrialist and, until recently, the head of one of the world's leading chemical companies, Roscoe Brunner felt deeply the struggle between worker and management and yet, for the first time in a long and eminent career, he was helpless, either to intervene or to influence. However, he had other reasons to remember 1926. These were personally far more traumatic and, in common with most everyone else, he would be glad to see the year's end.

A large black Daimler pulled alongside the kerb, the chauffeur stepping out effortlessly to open the door for Roscoe Brunner who climbed into the back seat. He was greeted by his wife, as affectionately as any man might expect after over a quarter of a century of married life, and on their way to Roehampton they chatted about the refurbishment of their new home, a grand mansion befitting the social status of a prominent London businessman which, of late, they had every reason to believe Roscoe Brunner would soon become. They may also have touched upon other issues, more emotive and more profound, concerning events surrounding one of the most bewildering, colossal mergers of British business interest ever undertaken.

Whatever the nature of their conversation in those few minutes' drive between the city centre and Roehampton, they seemed friendly and perfectly at ease as the chauffeur turned the limousine off Roehampton Lane and into the carriage drive of Green Cottage, the home of their daughter, Princess Shelagh, of the Royal House of Liechtenstein.

Princess Shelagh and her husband were away, enjoying an extended Continental holiday at their shooting lodge in the Austrian mountains, and Ethel Brunner, a talented and vivacious authoress, had taken personal charge of the household, as well as attending to the welfare of her baby grandson, Christopher.

At the front door of Green Cottage, Roscoe and Ethel Brunner were greeted by the maid who divested them of their outdoor apparel. Mrs Brunner ordered tea to be served in the first floor writing-room which, temporarily, doubled as her private bedroom. The coal shortage impinged upon everyone, even the wealthy.

Some minutes later, and after visiting their grandson in the nursery, the Brunners were settled in front of the writing-room fire and when the maid served their tea, everything appeared exactly as it should have been. Mr Brunner said he had an engagement in the city and would require the chauffeur at 8pm. His wife instructed that she would supper following his departure.

They never did either. Approximately three hours later, shortly before 10pm, on the evening of Wednesday November 3rd, 1926, the bodies of Roscoe and Ethel Brunner were discovered lying in a pool of blood in the Green Cottage writing-room. Ethel Brunner had been shot through the neck at close range whilst a single bullet through the temple had abruptly terminated her husband's life. In his hand he still clasped a tiny revolver.

To detectives, on the scene by midnight, it seemed obvious that Roscoe Brunner had murdered his wife and then taken his own life. But why?

Affluent and successful beyond the dreams of ordinary men and women of the 1920s, the Brunners appeared to have had everything to live for. Roscoe Brunner was one of the most respected figures in the British chemical industry; his wife was making a name for herself as an accomplished writer and together they enjoyed wealth, possessions and social standing. They were also blessed with two fine sons approaching manhood and a daughter married into European royalty.

Reports of the Roehampton tragedy hit the national headlines on the Friday morning and the business world, family, friends and politicians in high places were stunned as the newspapers left little to the imagination in their quest for the most salacious gossip behind the appalling tragedy:

> 'Secret of shot millionaire', 'Tragic quarrel over combine', 'A misguided wife', 'Millionaire's death in Prince's house', 'Secrets of mansion tragedy', 'A wife's indiscretions', 'Impulsive Lady Bountiful', 'Drama of high finance', '...the apparent eclipse of a magnate from his former eminent position'.

By the weekend, and to a column-inch, all of Fleet Street was of one steadfast opinion, that Roscoe Brunner had been driven to murder by his wife's interference in his business affairs following his demise from the chairmanship of the Brunner Mond chemical company and then his failure to secure a seat on the inaugural board of directors of the newly-created Imperial Chemical Industries (I.C.I.). Reported the Daily Mail:

> Although Mr Brunner felt the change in his fortunes, his wife took it even more to heart. She felt the alteration in her husband's commercial eminence so much that it obsessed her. He tried to pacify her, but apparently without success, and then came the formation of Imperial Chemical Industries. This new combine is to include Brunner Mond & Company as its largest component, but there is to be no place for Roscoe Brunner on the new board of directors. He

has been snubbed and his wife was known to be furious. She said he had not been treated fairly and, letting her anger get the better of her discretion, she made a round of visits to influential people with the object of trying to get her husband's grievances redressed. She visited people at their private houses, and at one, it is alleged, an unpleasant scene ensued. She went to newspaper offices and tried to arouse interest in her case, evidently moved by a deep-seated sense of grievance that in the constitution of the new board of directors no place had been found for her husband.

Though there did not appear to have been the slightest premeditation on the part of Roscoe Brunner, the wildest excesses of the press were brought into play and one newspaper, summing up the Brunners' marriage, declared that their former happy relations had snapped and '…there was continual bickering regarding Mrs Brunner's extravagance in the matter of entertainments, dress and other amusements'.

Others, not least the Daily Express, described Ethel Brunner as a 'highly-strung, temperamental woman' who had tried to dominate her husband. Another, perhaps delivering the coup de grace, revealed that six months earlier a celebrated West End clairvoyant had warned her 'good friend' Ethel Brunner that she was destined to meet a violent death. It was compulsive reading and London society was agog as each revelation unfurled, no matter from whatever dubious source it might have emanated.

The newspaper reporting subsequently proved critical and at the formal inquest, five days later, not one new shred of evidence was revealed beyond that which had been so colourfully painted in the 1920s' version of the modern tabloid press. Key witnesses were not called and information was withheld as the coroner, outraged by the media-inspired speculation, condemned the pre-inquest newspaper reporting as both indecent and improper. He complained that if just a one-hundredth part of the comment had been made in relation to a civil court action, then the editors would have been severely punished.

Precisely as directed, the jury formally returned verdicts of 'murder' and 'suicide whilst of unsound mind'; verdicts that were as straightforward and merciful as anyone closely connected with the Brunners could have hoped. Ethel Brunner's perceived interference in her husband's business affairs had made her a convenient scapegoat for the whole tragic affair.

Yet, as this investigation seeks to show, it was a beguiling lie, the product of a masterful public relations exercise in damage limitation that has since grown in substance to become fact, erroneously repeated in practically every I.C.I. history and official record that has ever been penned. What is concealed is an extraordinary saga of conflict, loyalty, treachery and a lust for power involving the Brunners and Sir Alfred Mond, boyhood friend and erstwhile business partner to Roscoe Brunner.

Sir Alfred Mond was an immensely wealthy autocrat who had once knocked on the door of greatness but never quite entered. He was a 'kingmaker', a personal friend to Lloyd George, and often a financier to the Lloyd George cause. He had risen to Ministerial rank, only to see his political ambitions crumble with the disintegration of the last great Liberal government. During the First World War, there were those who saw Mond as a fanatical patriot; others accused him of being a traitor and never before, or perhaps since, has a British political figure evoked such fierce emotion in his fellow countrymen and yet still succeeded in aspiring to high government office.

At the same time, and what is indisputable, is that Mond was one of the most dominant industrial figures of the century and as a political heavyweight and public benefactor he left an indelible mark on history. He made vast gifts to charity; he founded hospitals, promoted the founding of the British Imperial War Museum, organised the building of the Cenotaph, in London's Whitehall, and played an immeasurable role in the advancement of the Jewish free state of Israel.

He also built his own empire, Imperial Chemical Industries. It was his dream, his vision and when he ruthlessly set his mind to return from politics to industry his knife strokes were measured.

CHAPTER TWO
IN THE BEGINNING...

In Victorian England there was no port or city more responsive to the jetsam and flotsam of European society than Liverpool, the gateway to the New World. On October 23rd, 1868, in the nearby town of Widnes, a son, Alfred, was born to a gifted German scientist, Ludwig Mond and his wife Frida. From a family of Jewish silk merchants, Ludwig Mond had been attracted to England by the opportunities to make his fortune and, almost penniless but with valuable patents in his pocket, he had sailed on board a cattle boat from Rotterdam to seek a new life and he was soon employed at a Lancashire chemical works.

Here he struck up a friendship with the firm's office manager, John Brunner, the son of a Liverpool schoolteacher and with their families they took up residence in large neighbouring houses overlooking the great sprawl of Widnes which was then an abomination of the Industrial Revolution, a once marshy hamlet that had been transformed into a chemical manufacturing town where the foul air, the blackened landscape and the sinuous-streaked waters of the River Mersey was matched only by the human misery in the back-to-back houses of the labouring classes.

Lamented one contemporary writer: 'Those coming into Widnes, even from very dark and gloomy skies, enter the town with a certain awe and horror and wonder if life can actually be sustained'.

In 1865, John Brunner's wife, Salome, gave birth to their first son, John Fowler Brunner (Jack), and over the following five years she was blessed with the addition of three daughters and two additional sons, Sidney and Roscoe, the latter named after Henry Roscoe, a Professor of Chemistry at Owens College, Manchester.

Surrounded by their children, Salome Brunner and Frida Mond delighted in each other's company while their husbands went off to discuss their ideas for setting up in business together. Ludwig Mond, the pure scientist, knew the magic of discovery and he wanted to build a great works, a shrine to his inventions. John Brunner, on the other hand, countenanced caution and the need to ensure that balances would always be settled.

They had been considering a number of different chemical manufacturing processes and eventually settled for a new method of making soda ash, a primary raw material in the expanding glass, soap, paper and textile industries. They also decided to establish their new works on the tranquil tree-lined banks of the River Weaver, a tributary of the River Mersey, near to the Cheshire salt town of Northwich. The area was perfect, too perfect, in fact, and the powerful local landowners stood shoulder to shoulder in abhorrence and denial. Brunner and Mond could build their stinking chemical works anywhere, but not in the sacred precincts of Cheshire. The neighbouring chemical industry of Widnes was a horror, said the landowners. The soap and soda ash works belched thick black smoke day and night, and heavy with hydrochloric acid, it burnt hedges and destroyed crops. They argued that for every ton of soda ash made, double the weight of alkali waste was dumped and, rich in sulphur, it choked the little streams and polluted the Mersey itself. From this nauseating sludge seeped the odour of rotten eggs.

In the drawing rooms of the exalted there was talk of floggings and the setting of dogs on the miscreants and to make matters worse, neither Mond's rather fearsome appearance, nor his Continental manner were hardly likely to soften the county prejudice either. He was about 5ft-8ins tall, slightly stooped and always wore a black broad-brimmed, shapeless hat which half concealed a heavily bearded face, powerful racial nose and a much tortured and disfigured left eye, a lasting testimony to experiments with caustic soda.

With the spirit of Agincourt running through their veins, the Cheshire nobility, led by Lord Delamere, schemed and conspired to deprive the would-be business partners of the land they so desperately required. Brunner and Mond were furious as they prowled and probed for a weak point in the defences of the gentry until, finally, they discovered Winnington Hall with 130 acres of land, on the outskirts of Northwich. With brine, road, railway and a canalised river, it was probably the best site in all of England for their plans. Everyone had forgotten the eccentric diplomat, Lord Stanley, of Alderley, who owned the Winnington estate. He had been an absentee landlord for over twenty years and short of money he rented various corners to salt manufacturers, whilst the hall itself had become a ladies' finishing school or, as the headmistress put it, '...a school for the daughters of the gently born'. John Ruskin and Charles Halle were both honoured visitors at Winnington Hall and Ruskin had written to his father in 1859:

'This is such a fine place. I shall stay till Monday. The house stands in a superb park, full of trees and sloping down to the river. I like Mr Halle so very much. He was very happy yesterday evening, and actually played quadrilles for us to dance to...'.

Negotiations for the purchase of the Winnington estate dragged on for months because the partners were simply desperate for finance. They only wanted a portion of the land, but Lord Stanley insisted it was all or nothing and in the end they were mortgaged to the hilt to pay £16,000 for the hall and parkland. It left them vastly under-capitalised and in a precarious state.

Mond, tireless and pugnacious in pursuit of success, could not, would not, contemplate failure and even the normally cautious Brunner was prepared to press on, driven, no doubt, by a determination to cock a snoop at Lord Delamere and his cronies. Soon the chimneys and skeleton towers were beginning to dwarf Winnington Hall and its elegant parkland, Mond stamping over the broken earth, his great cigar puffing vigorously in his mouth as he cursed and spurred on his mainly Irish immigrant labourers. Local men, sceptical of the intimidating German and his motives, were as prejudiced as the landed gentry and refused point-blank to have anything to do with his accursed chemical works.

Immense problems arose in the early years of the soda ash manufacturing process but, in a mellowing climate of general acceptance, one or two local tradesmen agreed to provide enhanced credit and one local soap manufacturer even agreed to settle the payroll during a particularly fraught period.

'Everything that could break down, did break down, and everything that could burst, did burst,' remarked John Brunner. 'At the end of that fateful first fifteen months we had nothing left but our credit.'

In the midst of this technical strife, local animosity and financial hardship, John Brunner and Ludwig Mond moved their families into Winnington Hall, at the heart of their embryo chemical works. Hard and merciless, Mond would pace the works in a terrible rage. He was a German tyrant who frequently slept on the walkways above the plant, waiting for something to go wrong and petrifying his workforce.

'Heaven help the man who does his best and fails - for then there is no hope for him and I've no use for him,' he stormed.

When the great Winnington adventure had begun, Alfred Mond was still a few months short of his fifth birthday. His brother, Robert, was six, but there was no question as to who was the stronger character. It was Alfred who possessed their father's robustness and blunt nature and an inevitable clash of like-temperaments dominated the youngster's childhood, for in the Mond household there was only one master. Alfred came to be as suppressed as any hard-bitten worker by the fearsome stature and presence of his strong disciplinarian father who frowned upon him as something of a family fool. Just as with his men, Ludwig Mond demanded absolute obedience to his will and only in Robert could he see the flowering of his own ambitions and the hope of continued scientific genius.

The young Monds were raised in the strict enclave of a typical 19th century family; typical that is in as far as Ludwig and Frida remained staunchly German all of their lives and insisted upon the boys being attended by a German governess. The Monds despised Provincial England and Frida Mond also strongly disapproved of the English approach to education, so that when at home Robert and Alfred were allowed only to speak German. Even their books and play things were acquired from Germany and when it came to them attending weekly boarding school, they were sent to an establishment run by a Mr

Schelling, a hard and cold Prussian headmaster.

In the other wing of Winnington Hall, John Brunner, 'Papa', as he was affectionately known, doted on his children and amongst his large family he was able to relax away from the chronic difficulties which, more than once, saw the business on the verge of bankruptcy as it finally began producing soda ash, which then sold at a dismal loss of £5 per ton. Personal tragedy was also to impinge upon John Brunner at a time when his business acumen was more critically required than ever before. In the summer of 1874, his wife, Salome, died. Six children in nine years' of marriage had taken an exacting toll. The Brunner children were immediately whisked off to Liverpool to stay with Salome's parents whilst Brunner, temporarily, resided with the Monds, but he sorely missed his family and within a year he had remarried.

The second Mrs Brunner was Ethel Jane Wyman, the daughter of a Kettering physician and sister-in-law to Edward Nettleford, a Midlands' industrialist, with whom Brunner had business and social contacts. In turn, Nettleford was related to Joseph Chamberlain, the newly-appointed radical Liberal MP who was later to influence John Brunner's own political ambitions.

Frida Mond intensely disliked the second Mrs Brunner and made no secret of the fact that she disapproved of John Brunner marrying again so quickly, especially, as she put it, 'marrying his housekeeper'. She tried in vain to keep the Brunner and Mond boys apart, but in the rather surreal world of Winnington they grew up together, finding rich mischief in the endless steam pipes, furnaces and dark corners. They would steal the men's dinners and hide them, or pelt snow and turf at the office boy and fill the men's hats with lime; they would build dens down by the river and, in winter, skate on the ornamental pond. These were the precious childhood moments and shared experiences that so bond together men in later life.

By the time the Brunner and Mond boys were entering their teens, Winnington had become a much happier place. The size of the plant had doubled, output had trebled and, thanks to a combination of John Brunner's resourcefulness and Ludwig Mond's technical skills, each ton of soda ash was beginning to yield a profit.

It meant the two families could begin to enjoy the trappings of success and the five sons were all sent to be educated at Cheltenham College. Robert Mond was the one with a scientific leaning; Jack Brunner was the academic and Sidney and Roscoe Brunner the sportsmen and college prefects. The Brunner boys were altogether possessed of an easy charm that young Alfred Mond, attracted to the rugged English character, so desperately sought but never seemed able to attain. He had difficulty pronouncing the English language and, it was said, his clumsiness stood out in the cloistered confines of Cheltenham where he was distinguished by his foreignness. It was not much better upon his elevation with the Brunners to Cambridge where he showed little signs of the strength of character and forcefulness that was to mark him out in later life. He could speak perfect German, but he was shy, introspective, rather slovenly in appearance, and he quickly earned himself the name of 'Beau Mond'. As a conventional undergraduate at St. John's, it was said he was a failure, excelling only at poker.

Cambridge taught him, says his biographer, about the landed gentry and the rigid social system, but through it all he admired and envied the solid English character. He was determined that Englishness should not elude him indefinitely and his sights were firmly set on a career in politics. When his German cousins asked him what he meant to become, he had said simply: 'I shall be the Prime Minister of England'.

As a teenager at Cheltenham he had closely followed the progress of his father's partner, John Brunner who, in 1885, became the Member of Parliament for the Cheshire constituency of Northwich. A philanthropist and social reformer, with a record of caring for his workers through enhanced pay and conditions, education and welfare benefits, Brunner went on to represent Northwich for over twenty years, successfully defending for the Liberals in seven elections. He was created a Baronet in 1895 and by the turn of the century he was established as the Liberal Party's elder statesman.

John Brunner had been able to move into politics because, by the mid-1880s, the Brunner Mond business was beginning to flourish and, to an extent, was outgrowing the paternal management of its two founders. Brunner, an unusually self-effacing politician who put constituency and party before personal aspiration, continued to act as chairman, although his partner never openly approved of him dabbling in business and politics. Ludwig Mond had fallen out with the Liberals over their commitment to Irish Home Rule and, in any case, he was more concerned with scientific discoveries and the personal acquisition of some of the nation's art treasures.

In 1881, the Brunner Mond family business was formally registered as a limited company, with capital assets of £600,000, and though the founders kept a close watch on developments, especially those involving fundamental changes in commercial policy, the old order was giving way to the next generation. Jack, Sidney and Roscoe Brunner, and Robert and Alfred Mond, were being nurtured to hold in trust the ideals and principles established by their fathers. But it was not to be. Robert Mond, in the footsteps of his father, turned to new scientific horizons, whilst Alfred Mond made his position plain. His life's work was to be in politics, although it was in his wider interests to continue as a director of the company and, in part at least, to act as a proxy for his father.

As for the Brunners, young Jack Brunner also favoured politics and, after serving an apprenticeship as a councillor for Cheshire, he became an MP for the Liberals in Lancashire. Meanwhile, Sidney Brunner, never in the most robust of health, contracted life-threatening typhoid and whilst recuperating with the family in Italy, he drowned in a swimming accident. The natural business succession of the Brunner and Mond families had been severed and it was left to the youngest of the five sons, Roscoe Brunner, to emerge as the torch-bearer for the ageing founders' inveterate ambitions.

By this time, the whole of the British heavy chemical industry was in the hands of some forty or fifty manufacturers whose works were principally located on the saltfields of Cheshire and the neighbouring parts of Lancashire. Brunner Mond & Company stood at the head and when Roscoe Brunner left Cambridge he was able to contemplate a scene of prosperity, ripe for the picking for any young man, especially one whose father was joint founder and head of such a great concern. Barely out out of nappies when his natural mother died, Roscoe Brunner had been greatly influenced during his formative years by his strong-willed, church-going stepmother. From Ethel Jane Wyman he discovered social graces, a love of the opera, the fine things in life and a regard for his position as the son of a successful industrialist. From his Liberal Unitarian father he had learned the Victorian gospel of work, perseverance, application and a caring concern for his fellow man.

Unassuming, easy-going and generally 'one of the boys' amongst his contemporaries, Roscoe Brunner made a success of Cambridge and though qualified to be called to the Bar of London's Inner Temple, it was with the blessing of his father, and Ludwig Mond, that he turned to industrial management and day-to-day control of the company in Cheshire. At the same time, he too was increasingly pressured towards politics, but not for him a life at Westminster. Nevertheless, he was keenly interested in politics and was often at his father's side in some of the most fearsome of election battles in Cheshire when John Brunner was denounced for his trade relations, his theological convictions and his partnership with a German Jew. The most famous of John Brunner's campaigns occurred at an important by-election in 1887 and it was to have momentous consequences for the future life of young Roscoe.

John Brunner was contesting the Northwich seat for the Gladstonian Liberals against the Duke of Westminster's son, Lord Henry Grosvenor, a Liberal Unionist, whom he attacked for his social privilege and his narrow class interest. However, on this occasion the election had little to do with personalities for it was dominated by the single, controversial issue of Irish Home Rule. The pundits argued that there had never been a clearer choice between the opposing policies of coercion and conciliation, and no constituency was seen to be more representative of English society as a whole than Northwich. Brunner was an ardent Irish Home Ruler and defeat for both himself and his leader, William Gladstone, was unthinkable. For Grosvenor and the Liberal Unionists it would be a disaster and the general feeling was that it would lead to a break-up of the Empire.

Reports of the by-election appeared daily in the press and many eminent politicians flocked to the town in a frenzied attempt to influence votes. Seldom had a mid-term contest caused such a sensation and, long before the days of opinion polls, the analysts pored over the outcome. Polling took place on a Saturday and there was an anxious wait for the count on the following Monday when John Brunner, with his family at his side, was duly returned as Member of Parliament for Northwich. The news spread like the proverbial wildfire throughout the country and across to Ireland where, said the Manchester Guardian, '... all Dublin was thrown in ecstasy by the Northwich result and the streets of the city rang with the cry of victory'.

Westminster too was abuzz with the news which was seen as a strong condemnation of Government policy. The Prime Minister, Lord Salisbury, was advised, on the strength of Brunner's victory, to tender his resignation to Queen Victoria, but history shows that he survived amid uproar as the euphoria of Ireland gave way to bloodshed.

Inevitably, John Brunner came to be a frequent visitor and speaker in Dublin and it was here that he struck up a close friendship with Dr Arthur Houston Q.C who shared his dream of an Irish Free State. A Doctor of Law at Dublin University, Houston was persuaded to enter mainstream British politics and Brunner sought a possible seat for him within his own sphere of the North West of England and when a General Election was called he was officially adopted as the Liberal candidate for Warrington, the nearest main town to Brunner's Northwich constituency. In Warrington, the voters were presented with a straight choice; the Irish Liberal, or a local brewer, Robert Pierpoint, for the Conservatives. Dr Houston did better than expected, but fell to a small Conservative majority amidst Liberal complaints that at least sixty-five voters in one ward were noted to be intoxicated. Dr Houston left Warrington with the words ringing in his ears that the town would be represented by one who was tied to the beer barrels.

Undeterred by this election setback, John Brunner and Dr Houston became even closer allies in championing the cause of Irish Home Rule. They were also friends and frequently holidayed with each other, in Dublin, London or Liverpool, the latter where Brunner had settled away from the hurly burly of Winnington Hall. The two families were often together and, encouraged by their respective fathers, a romance grew and blossomed between Brunner's dashing and genial son, Roscoe, and Dr Houston's mercurial daughter, Ethel. Roscoe's charm, personality and wealth had marked him out as an ideal husband amongst local society families seeking a 'good catch', the early days of Brunner Mond's 'stinking works' long forgotten.

Still only seventeen, Ethel was the eldest of three Houston daughters, a fiercely independent young woman, headstrong, tempestuous and nurtured to seek for herself the best station in life. From her mother she had inherited a talent for music and the theatre, and from her father a passion for justice and fairness and with youth in her heart, she wanted to change the world. Roscoe Brunner was captivated by her beauty and the mystique of Irishness, but he knew full well that she was never likely to become the archetypal Victorian wife, languid at her needlework, simpering fetchingly at his side and happy to bask in the glory of his status and success. Cast in the mould of those of her day who were about to emancipate the lot of all womenfolk in Britain, she was so very much her own woman and, as she proved in later life, she possessed the strength of will to match and even surmount most of the men around her.

Their courtship was often fiery, the epitome some would say of a perfect partnership; she strong-willed and ambitious; he carefree, happy and content in the knowledge that family wealth and an abiding sense of duty would be sufficient to carry him through life.

They were married, a few days before Christmas in 1898, at Christ Church, Paddington, London, and afterwards Roscoe Brunner established himself as the founders' voice at the head of the company and over 50,000 workers worldwide. It was a role that suited him well and from director level to labourer's lackey he was well liked and respected.

To reflect his standing as one of the district's most prominent businessmen, Roscoe Brunner searched for a suitable home, somewhere spacious and grand where he could bring up his young family. The new industrial wealth of the early 20th century was in the hands of the likes of the Brunners and Monds and when Roscoe and Ethel came upon Belmont Hall, in the sleepy village of Great Budworth, near to Northwich, they found their grand home. Indicative of the new age, they negotiated a lease from a local ancestral landowner who had chosen to move to less commodious surrounds.

A mansion of two centuries, Belmont Hall stood strong, dignified and opulent. It contained splendid works of art and suites of stately rooms and it could comfortably accommodate upwards of one hundred dinner guests. From the drawing room, Roscoe Brunner was able to look out across the Weaver valley and Winnington works, whilst for his wife Belmont Hall was somewhere to impress, to organise lavish dinner parties and to entertain liberally the important dignitaries and lords and ladies who now paid homage to the success of the huge local enterprise of Brunner Mond & Company. Ethel Brunner's charity work, her support of 'good causes' and her tireless efforts on behalf of her chosen political party had no equal in the district and soon she was enjoying the status of the 'Lady Bountiful of Belmont Hall', a position which the established, well-heeled ladies of the Cheshire set bore with not a little resentment.

Hers was 'new money' and they viewed her with a considerable degree of suspicion and, at times, downright animosity. To them she was an Irish interloper, without breeding, and she traded on her position and her wealth. More to the point, they were probably jealous of her independence.

Ludwig Mond

John Brunner

The Hollies, Widnes, birthplace of Alfred Mond

Winnington Hall School

CHAPTER THREE
MOND AND POLITICS

Alfred Mond was determined to follow John Brunner into Parliament. Since the days of his youth he had been entranced by the gossip from Westminster and at every opportunity he would waylay Brunner to discuss politics. They would chat about the great men who ran the country, the ideals that flourished among the young politicians and the dangerous excitement of elections. John Brunner had come to be regarded as a figure of great stature in the Liberal Party and though he fired Alfred Mond's ambitions, they often found themselves with diametrically opposed political views. Brunner was a strong Radical, but a 'Little Englander', whose limitations held scant charm for Mond. Brunner, with some poignancy, frequently declared that though he did not particularly dislike his partner's son, he just did not trust him.

Following what was a dismal performance at Cambridge, Mond managed to patch up his mistakes at Edinburgh University and, for a time, he toyed with a legal career as a barrister on the Chester & North Wales circuit, but his heart was not in it and when, in 1897, he became Managing Director of Brunner Mond & Company, at its London office, it seemed infinitely more appealing to the stuffiness of a life in chambers. More significantly, it allowed him to visit Westminster and to begin rubbing shoulders with the new young Liberal bloods. His wealth and his connections were soon serving him well and in the Khaki election of 1900 he stood for the Liberals, in Salford.

His growling voice, his abrasiveness and his foreign tongue, which always seemed to display traits of perceived bitterness, hardly endeared him to the Lancastrian artisans and defeat was assured when he began to further prejudice his chances by flying the Temperance flag. It was merely a setback, for Mond was already building friendships with an even more powerful circle of political allies, not least of them David Lloyd George, the fire and brimstone Welsh MP who liked to surround himself with the new Liberal force of 'self-made business-men'. These included the Warrington MP Arthur Crosfield, the son of a soap manufacturer who had helped with Brunner Mond's payroll in the early troubled years; Charles Henry, an energetic Jewish Australian; and Timothy Davies, the prosperous mayor of Fulham. As is the way in politics, their loyalty was eventually rewarded with Parliamentary seats and, subsequently, titles.

In 1892, Alfred Mond married Violet Goetze, the daughter of a London commercial family, and at their wedding Roscoe Brunner stood as best man. The Goetzes were of German extraction, though English for several generations, and Violet, with an irrepressible charm and an agile mind, was just the woman to help Mond achieve his political aspirations. She led an active life as a hostess and organiser and together with their political friends, including Lloyd George, they socialised freely, often spending tennis weekends at the Highgate country home of Arthur Crosfield. These occasions attracted a host of influential people, like the MPs Arthur Balfour, who always asked for new balls to help his eyesight, and F.E.Smith (later Lord Birkenhead) who drank a 'bottle of fizz' before the game, apparently because it 'helped his vision'. Mond was very much a part of this inner circle and inseparable over many years as a golfing partner to Lloyd George and Crosfield. On one memorable occasion, when all three were serving Members of Parliament, they were playing together on Mond's private course when Lloyd George was accosted by two women disguised in masculine attire.

'Give women the vote, you wicked man,' they shrieked.

'Go away. We're playing golf,' roared Lloyd George, taking up a defensive stance.

It was with much relief that the two intruders then revealed themselves as Violet Mond and Crosfield's wife, Domini.

Mond's money and his friendships served him well and in the 1906 General Election he was chosen to contest Chester for the Liberals. A bulwark of Conservatism and only twenty miles from Brunner Mond's main chemical works, it was an ancient walled Roman town whose citizens viewed industrial areas as vulgar, innovation as indecent. For close on two decades they had been represented by Squire Yerburgh, a country gentleman whose own family story stretched into antiquity. Cestrians knew Yerburgh and they mistrusted 'the foreigner' Mond, a Jew who actually sent his wife knocking on doors to canvass their support. Mond, with guidance from the master orator Lloyd George, swept through the Cheshire county town on a wave of passion, personally supported by the Prime Minister, Sir Henry Campbell Bannerman who furthered the cause in front of a huge rally chaired by Mond's political mentor, John Brunner.

The poll, in early January, could hardly have been closer. In a scene of high drama, the returning officer was on the verge of declaring Yerburgh the victor when Mond insisted there had been a mistake in the counting. Stepping forward he searched bundles of voting papers and found a batch wrongly accredited to his opponent. The margin was so narrow that this single bundle ensured Alfred Mond became the new Member of Parliament for Chester, by just forty-seven votes.

Afterwards, Lloyd George commented: 'They were afraid of Mond at first, but he stood up before them and the force of his silence was enough to keep them quiet. And then he spoke, with knowledge which was simple and in phrases which were expressive. His sincerity broke down the resentment. They listened to the message of Liberalism. When he was moved by his own thought, he was effective, so much so that you forgot his accent. There were no gestures. His hands were still at his side. There was just the glow of Mond's intelligence - that was all ! And yet it was not all! There was an intensity which carried the Chester men with him.'

Mond was no stranger when he took his seat as one of 377 Liberals in the new Parliament under what was regarded as a brilliant team of Ministers headed by Campbell-Bannerman and with Herbert Asquith as the Chancellor of the Exchequer, R.B.Haldane at the War Office, Lord Morley at the India Office and Lloyd George as President of the Board of Trade. Mond had made it his business to mix with men of Cabinet rank, or near-Cabinet rank, and his acquaintances included the likes of Herbert Gladstone, Lord Tweedmouth, the Earl of Crewe and the rising young Ministers, Reginald McKenna, Herbert Samuel and Winston Churchill. These were the new 'middle class' representatives, men of means who outstripped the Tories in wealth.

Mond felt deeply his own speech inadequacies and so, day after day, he walked up and down his study in London's Lowndes Square, struggling with elocution lessons in preparation for his maiden speech, on Chinese labour in Africa. It was of little interest to the House, but when he began arguing the cause of Free Trade there were howls of protest from the Conservatives. To them, Mond was another Jew who through some cleverness of his race, had amassed a fortune.

Meanwhile, Brunner Mond had become one of the most powerfully represented companies in the land, with three of its senior directors all sitting in Parliament for the Liberals - Sir John Brunner (made a Baronet in 1895), his son Jack Brunner and not least, Alfred Mond.

Back in Cheshire, Roscoe Brunner continued to manage the company with a steady hand, steering it ever onwards to more success as he rigorously pursued a policy of enlargement and expansion. The family Mond, though still represented on the board of directors and, collectively, retaining substantial ownership, had been gently pushed aside on matters of policy and even the ageing Dr Ludwig Mond was left in the slipstream of development. To consult him, admitted Sir John Brunner to Alfred Mond, was often a painful process. 'Finding that matters put before him were dealt with slowly... I had to decide to report things as done,' remarked Sir John.

In 1909, Dr Mond, the fearsome German chemist who had conquered all to establish the business, died and Alfred Mond thanked Sir John for the way in which he had looked after his father's interests in the latter years - '...for taking the management of our business out of my father's hands'.

More to the point, as Sir John almost certainly recognised, Alfred Mond was resentful of the Brunner family's control of the company and, with a significant chunk of his father's shares to add to his own considerable holding, he was going to be a dangerous bedfellow.

And so it came to pass, for within days of his father's death, Alfred Mond was visiting Sir John, to request a stronger voice for the Mond family in the running of the company. What he wanted was a surrogate role on the board for his cousin, Emile Mond, who would then be able to '...know officially what he knows privately'. It was also Alfred Mond's way of ensuring that, while a serving MP and residing in London, he would be kept minutely informed and Sir John did not like the idea. He reported to Roscoe Brunner that it had been a friendly meeting, but he did not feel kindly disposed to the suggestion. A rift was developing between the founding Brunner and Mond families and only Sir John survived to hold together the last remnants of co-operation and unity.

In politics Alfred Mond had quickly become recognised as an accomplished Parliamentarian, excelling in the turmoil of Liberalism as Campbell-Bannerman gave way to Asquith as the new Prime Minister, with Lloyd George as Chancellor of the Exchequer. Asquith, British to the core, sat and viewed Mond critically as he had viewed Disraeli and the Prince Consort. To him they were all foreigners and his feelings for anybody from the other side of the English Channel were tinged with patronising pity. Mond's view of his leader was one of equal pity, for although he reasoned that Asquith had a fine brain, '...he was incapable of presenting a problem to itself, whereas if a problem was presented to it by someone else, they got a good result'.

Not surprisingly, in the reshuffling of office in 1910, Asquith rather condescendingly told Mond: 'The Ministerial jobs have been promised and you are too big a man for an under-secretaryship.'

Mond was bitterly disappointed and not even Lloyd George, who for the time being had pushed him as far as possible, could intervene. By way of recompense, a Baronetcy was conferred upon Mond, but it was an honour that probably had more to do with his hefty support for the Liberals' war chest rather than political performance during the few years in which he had been a Member of Parliament. Indeed, even the saintly Gladstone had been known to sell titles in return for secret contributions and it is well documented that later, Lloyd George, more brazenly, organised a regular tariff of £10,000 for a Knighthood, £25,000 for a Baronetcy and £100,000 for a Peerage. So Mond became Sir Alfred Mond (Bart.) and also a Right Honourable Member of the

Privy Council.

Meanwhile, across Europe in the land of Mond's forefathers, the German nation was ominously expanding its battle fleet and as Britain looked on with foreboding, Lloyd George began to implement a massive counter-balance. Dreadnought battleships were to be the Admiralty's response and Lloyd George's answer was to finance their building through a series of sweeping new taxes. The Conservative Party fiercely opposed him and when the Budget reforms reached the House of Lords they were rejected amidst cries of 'constitutional crisis'. Lloyd George was furious and Sir Alfred Mond joined in the attack on their Lordships, although some MPs had reason to wonder at the hypocrisy of the man, for if anyone might have been perceived as a member of the privileged class it was he.

Unmoved by the sniping, Mond publicly denounced the House of Lords as a High Tory committee operating at a snail's pace. Many years later, and like so many MPs with nowhere else to go in politics, Mond was happy to embrace the House of Lords.

As in industry and business, Mond was altogether impatient with the prevarications of the British system which he described as 'the habit of waiting until things happen, the complete neglect to endeavour to foresee possible difficulties - the most popular of British systems, known as muddling through.'

His foreign tongue, his well known admiration for German methods and organisation, and sometimes his urge to force an efficient Teutonic regime on those around him, often antagonised his opponents, particularly the Conservatives and, occasionally, the old guard in the Liberal Party. A fellow Parliamentarian, exasperated with his references to European ideals, rebuked him:

'I am not concerned very much with what occurs abroad. I am an Englishman and, rightly or wrongly, I believe that England is the first country in the world, and I am quite content to go upon the old lines my forefathers went on before. What was good enough for them is good enough for me.'

Mond was not generally popular and he was seldom trusted. One of his fiercest opponents said of him: 'He is a seer of visions, a weaver of dreams'. Others saw him as no more than a 'bloated Plutocrat right down to his fat cigar', but whatever his personal and visionary capabilities, he was not a politician, or a businessman for that matter, to ignore. Those who tried, did so at their peril.

So with the House of Lords rejecting Lloyd George's Budget, Prime Minister Asquith advised King Edward VII to dissolve Parliament. A General Election was decreed and Mond, the Imperialist and the ardent Free Trader, took the fight to his new Liberal 'safe haven' of Swansea which was further reward for his personal loyalty and wealth in support of the Lloyd George cause.

In order to force his financial reforms through the House of Commons, Lloyd George had established what came to be known as the 'Budget League', a sort of powerful unofficial arm of the Whip's office, and though Lloyd George himself had no formal connection, it was said that he personally attended to the finances. This created considerable friction with some members of the Liberal Party, including the forthright MP, Jack Pease who accused Lloyd George, to his face, of promising honours in support of the 'Budget League'. Whether or not this is true, the Manchester Guardian journalist Harry Spender, who served twenty-five years as Lloyd George's agent, named Sir Alfred Mond as one of the largest contributors and, certainly, shortly afterwards, Mond was elevated to the Baronetage. Lloyd George had much to thank him for and when he went to Swansea to speak to his countrymen, he declared:

'Mr Mond is known to every member of the House of Commons as one of the ablest members. There is no man in the House who has delivered speeches on behalf of Free Trade which have been more effective than those of Mr Mond.'

Opposing Mond was an indefatigable trade unionist, Ben Tillet, who roared defiance: 'The only reason this Mond is asked to represent you is because this Mond has plenty of money.'

Mond's methods, he said, were sordid, wicked, calumnious and dirty, and the best course of action would be to throw him into the docks. Responding more subtly by threatening to put his opponent in the stocks, or on a charge of libel, Mond prevailed without resorting to either extreme, although, presumably to hit back at his detractors, he did try to buy the business of one of the local newspapers, the South Wales Voice.

Stamping into the office of the owner/editor, Ebenezer Rees, Mond put his cheque book on the desk and said: 'Rees, name your figure. I want your paper and works, lock stock and barrel. I want to ensure that I get back into the House. Your paper will be my platform.'

Old Rees was unmoved. 'I'm not selling, Mond,' he retorted and in doing so he gained for himself the reputation of being one of the few men in Wales ever to say 'no' to Mond's money.

Nationally, the Liberals did no more than hold their ground. Before the end of the year, the continuing conflict escalated between the House of Commons and the Lords and though Mond's former mentor, Sir John Brunner, had retired from Westminster, he was not out of politics. His name headed a list of two hunded and fifty prospective Liberal Peers who were to be elevated by Asquith if their Lordships refused to give way on Lloyd George's Budget. He was destined to become Lord Everton, a dubious honour in his opinion and he wrote to his son, Roscoe Brunner:

'I saw Alec Murray (Liberal Chief Whip) last Thursday and told him frankly and plainly that I wanted no reward for what I had done, that if he wanted men to carry the Bill in the Lords, I would go there with joy, but that if it were merely the granting of honours I should prefer to be left out. If the passage of the new Bill were absolutely assured they would present to the King a short-list of highly distinguished men with myself at the head. My main reason for hanging back is the fear that my grandsons would grow up to be snobs.'

It was typical of Sir John who remained a self-professed Lloyd George man. They were both from a non-conformist background and they both had a disdain for inherited privilege. Sir John was pressed from all sides to accept a Peerage and both his sons, Jack and Roscoe, were in favour, the latter vociferously supported by his wife. Indeed, Ethel Brunner could see new rungs on the social ladder if she was to become the daughter-in-law of a peer of the Realm. Fortunately for Sir John, the crisis passed and his escape was executed. His honour lay in becoming President of the National Liberal Federation.

'Verily, the House of Lords is a snobbish institution,' he wrote to Roscoe Brunner.

But then, wouldn't his daughter-in-law have loved it?

The unveiling of a life-like bronze statue of Ludwig Mond, outside Winnington Hall, in Cheshire, was symbolic of a passing age and a changing world. Old Mond, dustcoat, felt hat and holding a bundle of plans in his hand, seemed to be gazing out for all eternity, as Sir Alfred Mond would have said, 'viewing the future from the plateau of history'.

Ludwig Mond's death had begun to bring down the final curtain on the old order through which the Brunner and Mond families had jointly held power for forty years.

In 1913, there was great upheaval and uncertainty everywhere, not only across Europe but domestically as well, for Roscoe Brunner and his fellow directors. There were huge expansions for Brunner Mond & Company to finance, £2 million worth of shares to sell and bitter acrimony to settle with one of the company's fiercest rivals. In the political arena, Sir John Brunner had vied for many years with the soap manufacturing magnate Sir William Hesketh Lever for the distinction of being the Liberal Party's chief benefactor. Brunner effectively came out on top in mere skirmishes of what was to follow as the respective companies of these two headstrong men lurched towards open warfare. Roscoe Brunner, as titular head of Brunner Mond, controlled most business dealings, but in all matters involving his old adversary, Sir John had much to settle and forcibly took his stance as company chairman, though rather than sound business rationale he may have been driven by an intense dislike of his rival; a feeling mutually returned by William Hesketh Lever who was the autocratic head of Lever Brothers, the world's leading makers of soap.

In 1907 and 1911, Lever had reluctantly entered into contracts for the supply of alkali from Brunner Mond; alkali being an indispensable raw material in producing soap. Brunner Mond held almost a monopoly in alkali in the home market and, indirectly, in Europe as well, so Sir John and Roscoe Brunner were able to bargain until the pips literally squeaked. Sir John saw Lever as a potential competitor and a threat to his own markets, but Lever despised their agreements, not that they impinged duly upon his own soap-making business, but more as a matter of personal pride. On one notable occasion, he stormed at Roscoe Brunner that he was not a Brunner Mond office clerk to be pushed about and told how to run his business. The upshot of the agreements barred Lever from entering into the alkali business and, in return, Brunner Mond gave an undertaking not to sell alkali to anyone more cheaply than it did to Lever Brothers. It meant that Brunner Mond and Levers were locked into what was to become a monumental business struggle.

Hesketh Lever, like Sir John Brunner, was a self-made man and not one to indulge too long in self-pity and when the opportunity arose he quickly took precautionary measures, in good time for the day when the Brunners would return with a new contract. To this end he purchased 1,700 acres of salt-bearing land in Cheshire and with it the ability to begin the manufacture of alkali in his own right. Naturally, this was instantly perceived as a challenge to Brunner Mond and Sir John instigated retaliatory measures by purchasing Joseph Crosfield & Sons and William Gossage & Sons, the two largest soap firms in opposition to Lever Brothers. This was ostensibly to protect Brunner Mond's marketplace and Lever was backed into an even tighter corner with his main competitors united behind the industrial muscle of his great rivals.

The battle lines were drawn and Brunner Mond and Levers entered into protracted and bitter negotiations which eventually resulted in a complicated new agreement involving the shares of Crosfields and Gossages, which Sir John Brunner had clearly never intended to be anything more than mere bargaining chips.

At this time, Sir Alfred Mond had little influence over what was going on with Levers; Sir John Brunner saw to that, but to Mond's political sensibilities the row was a typical British business squabble, petty and shortsighted and certainly not likely to benefit any of the parties involved. He wrote to Roscoe Brunner:

'...the head of the soap departments of Crosfields, Gossages and

Levers have been fighting for years and will continue to fight and to make difficulties unless we decide not to permit them.'

From Hesketh Lever's point of view, Brunner Mond was never likely to be a conciliatory influence and by the outbreak of the First World War, in 1914, the whole conflict had plummeted into personal venom and not even the slaughter being enacted on the battlefields of France could deter the rivalling factions. A new agreement of 1913 had brought about a temporary truce by granting Lever's company a half interest in both Crosfields and Gossages, but the ceasefire held only briefly and for the major part of the war years, the two protagonists became as entrenched as the battle lines on the Somme. Hesketh Lever was not content to be a bit-part player and he wanted Crosfields and Gossages for himself.

Such were the complexities that when the acrimony inevitably spilled over into the courts, one officiating judge openly admitted that he could not make much sense of the interminable quarrelling and he dismissed the case, hoping that Messrs Brunner Mond and Levers could resume normal business relations without any further trace of bitterness. In the end, Brunner Mond agreed to sell Crosfields and Gossages to Lever Brothers, but at an inflated price of £4 million. Hesketh Lever was outraged and he never forgot the £1 million that he thought he was overcharged and the repercussions for the Brunner and Mond families were to be unimaginable.

Beau' Mond (second left)...poker at Cambridge.

Alfred Mond electioneering in Chester.

CHAPTER FOUR
DISTANT WAR DRUMS

I f one figure stood out as an enigma above all others in British politics at the outbreak of the Great War, it was Sir Alfred Mond. He was a British Member of Parliament, a Privy Counsellor, a Baronet and yet he was of German stock and proud of his heritage. The European crisis, therefore, grieved him more than most, although his unique position also presented opportunities for him to air his views on Anglo-German relations in both countries and on the eve of war, in the German magazine, Nord und Sud, he was imploring co-operation and restraint:

> England is Germany's largest customer... In these circumstances it is difficult to conceive how it can be contended that England is jealous of Germany's industrial development, as surely a businessman is always glad when he sees a good customer placed in a position to give him large orders... It is most unreasonable that the two countries should rend each

other for the advantage of their rivals... Any interruption of trade between them would unquestionably result for both of them in a huge industrial and financial crisis.

Hysterical incitements to war and the crushing financial burden of armaments, understandably, had no place in Mond's reasoning. His personal dilemma was profound. If Germany and Britain were to be at one another's throats, where did his own loyalties lie? A radical pacifist, as was Lloyd George in the years preceding the war, he was a man of immense stature and wealth, still a rather forbidding, stiff personality, but comfortably settled into the Englishness that he so often despaired of attaining in his younger life, and he had purchased a magnificent country house, Melchet Court, in Hampshire, set within one thousand acres of parkland adjoining the New Forest.

In business, away from Brunner Mond & Company, he had developed other successful companies in nickel and gas and had even dabbled in the press, taking a major controlling interest in the Westminster Gazette, a London circulation Liberal daily newspaper. Furthermore, for a politician of only eight years standing, he had also made great strides towards Government office. The influential publication, Truth, wrote:

> There is no finer sight in creation than the member for Swansea, standing in a full House with a beaming smile on his face, while he instructs Mr Bonar Law on the multiplication table and the geography of Canada. Somebody once said that it was intellect talking through the nose - a description too accurate to be quite kind. Not that Sir Alfred Mond would object, for it is one of his virtues that he is entirely indifferent to petty personal insults. Knowledge, he would say, need not be pretty; it is power, especially when you get a patent before talking about it, and power without prettiness is the essential quality of Sir Alfred Mond's statesmanship. He is ready, like John Wesley, to take the whole world for his parish, or, as he would more humbly express it, his

market. His mind works with childlike simplicity. All he does is map out the solar system, and say to his competitors, 'Why should we be greedy? You take one continent - take it, by all means - and I'll be content with the rest'. If he were at Downing Street, there would brood over all the Empire a thoroughly up-to-date benevolence. Sir Alfred Mond would be the Universal Secretary of State, with Consols at a premium. And if Germany became restive he would say, blandly, 'I know Germany better than the right hon. and hon. gentlemen opposite'. (Loud ironical cheers.) .

Just days before the official declaration of war, and almost to the hour of Germany's ultimatum to France and Russia, Mond's Westminster Gazette was demanding that Britain should keep out of the looming crisis, comment which was quickly seized upon by every major newspaper in Germany. The following day the Westminster Gazette went further by publishing information which, it stated, was 'formally authorised by the German Foreign Office', which, in fact, meant authorised by the high-minded and peace-loving German ambassador, Prince von Lichnowsky.

This was clearly calculated to support Germany's intentions against France and Russia and, at such a critical moment in history, Mond was perceived in most quarters to have been behind the edito-

David Lloyd George and Violet Goetze

rial stance, although he would doubtless have argued that his desire to foster peace and friendship with Germany was consistent with the neutralists in the sharply divided Liberal Party.

The outbreak of war, on August 4th, brought forth the Gazette's most impassioned plea for Britain to protect the 'Germans within our gates', i.e. all German nationals residing in Britain, even those suspected of espionage. Of course, as Mond was himself of German origin, the newspaper's motives were immediately held to ridicule. War with any other country would have given Mond greater opportunities and prestige, but within a few days he was in danger of being swept away in a tidal wave of nationalistic fervour.

He was a symbol of all that was malevolent to the British nation, i.e from German stock and a Jew, and the fanaticism erupted over him when a national newspaper discovered that his second forename was Moritz, and printed it, with a statement that the British workman did not want 'Sir Alfred Moritz Mond' to cry out for him.

According to his biographer, a friend of power and influence visited Mond and implored him to leave the political arena, to retire to the country and wait for the war to end. Other Germans in high places were taking this course and Mond would be advised to do the same, but then rich men, like pretty women, seldom recognise the truth.

'You can all go to hell,' exclaimed Mond. 'I won't go into the country. I shall go into the Government instead.'

There were protests against him everywhere as London throbbed with the excitement of the war declaration. People pressed against the railings of Buckingham Palace, the newspaper headlines screamed hysteria and Mond went about his business, unperturbed. His speeches became more bellicose, he turned Melchet Court into a hospital, his London home into a haven for Belgian refugees and his son, Henry, went to fight in France, an officer with the South Wales Borderers.

'I say for God's sake let us all join to win the war, and when we have won it there will be time enough, if we have the inclination, to return to the quarrels of the past. We have to realise our enemy's cunning; there has been too much killing our opponent with the mouth instead of the bullet.'

It made little difference. To the public at large, Sir Alfred Mond was a German and not to be trusted and the charges continued to mount against him. Letters of hatred, letters of accusation continued to flood through his door and as early as the first winter of the war he was forced, with Sir John Brunner, to take legal action against a Leicester paper merchant who wrote to them:

'Those German Swine, Rt. Hon. Sir John Brunner, MP, and Sir Alfred Mond MP - Hope you are satisfied with the devastation and misery caused by your fellow Hogs in Belgium and France.'

Sir John, by birth half Swiss and half Manx, and without a drop of German blood in his veins, had every reason to be outraged. His German associations went no further than having been in business with Ludwig Mond, and now his son. The law suit was successful and the defendant was ordered to apologise and pay costs.

Mond rode the storm and on went the war. The troops were not home for Christmas and misery piled upon anguish as the politicians at Westminster fought out their own differences. Asquith's Coalition Government teetered on the brink of disaster and as founder of a Liberal 'ginger group' tasked with bringing Lloyd George to power, Mond argued fervently that his friend and political ally was the only man who could lead Britain from the abyss. Asquith's dithering diplomacy had been a failure and when, towards the end of 1916, Lloyd George rose in the House of Commons, Britain was ready for a new, demanding, vigorous Ministry. 'Diplomacy be damned, let us have results,' thundered Lloyd George.

It was a defining moment in the war and Mond was singled out to join the new administration in an act of what appeared to be incredible ambivalence. Lloyd George, a special champion of a vigorous patriotism and the elimination of all traces of German influence, was out for popularity and he cannot have believed that Mond was a popular investment.

'There was nearly a Conservative revolt when I put him (Mond) in the Government,' Lloyd George recalled years later. 'I was also putting Winston Churchill into the Government and Bonar Law (the Conservative Party leader) said to me, 'You can't put them both in. I don't know whether we will survive'. Winston Churchill's failure over the Dardanelles was still remembered and the Conservatives said that Mond was a German Jew.'

And so it was that Sir Alfred Mond became First Commissioner of Works, the highest office that even Lloyd George dared confer upon his old friend, for of all the monstrously rich men he courted at this time, Mond, with his German connections, his name and his ancestry, must surely have been the one he least welcomed. The enormity of the task facing the Government, and its demand for men of a unique business calibre, certainly favoured Mond, but no-one could believe for a second that his appointment, in the midst of war, was not at least part reward for past loyalties and his financial support of Lloyd George.

Within less than two years of Lloyd George accepting the Premiership of Great Britain, the war was over. In London, the sirens screamed, the guns thundered and the streets were awash with hysterical cheering crowds. It was the Armistice, it was victory, the victory to end all wars. Great Britain had paid dearly in the lives of one million men and the survivors, five million of them, demanded a land fit for heroes. In the House of Commons, Sir Alfred Mond stood with his fellow MPs to welcome Lloyd George who read out the terms of the Armistice.

'This is no time for words. Our hearts are too full of gratitude, to which no tongue can give adequate expression,' said the Prime Minister.

At the end of the war, Mond was in charge of many of the arrangements for the peace celebrations and he oversaw a number of major public works' projects, including completion of the British War Museum and Sir Edwin Lutyens' Cenotaph, in Whitehall, and when the post-war 'Khaki Election' came, he once more went to Swansea, as a Lloyd George 'Coupon' man, to be returned with a slender majority. Soon he was back to the office he had held since 1916, that of First Commissioner of Works, but with the war over, day-to-day mundane matters began to exasperate him and he was often guilty of impulsive eccentricity, as on the occasion when a deputation of serious men visited him at Whitehall. Mond listened to the arguments set before him, seldom looking up at the group. Suddenly he leapt to his feet, picked up his hat and went out. Somebody had made one statement which excited him and he had taken the phrase with him into the street, to cogitate upon it, totalling forgetting to return. But whatever else he was, Mond remained, down to his fat cigar, a capitalist and he brought out the fiercest emotions in his opponents. Describing him at this time as a 'rather flamboyant specimen of a certain class of very rich men', the magazine Everyman commented:

> Sir Alfred Mond would pass unnoticed if he were simply a great landlord seeking a garter, or a mere man of wealth after a barony. But he is more than that. He is a very pushful and skilful hand at the political game, working for the most part behind the scenes, and fully alive to the importance of the newspaper as a weapon. He is immensely rich, acute, cynical, and probably knows quite well what he wants...

Depressed by the routine and tradition of his Ministerial post, Mond told Lloyd George that he wished to return to industry, a decision that his fiercest critics reasoned was, in part, due to Germany's crushing defeat and the floundering of his own personal ambitions. Others thought it was an astute political manoeuvre to cajole Lloyd George into granting him high Ministerial Office, though what this did not recognise was that Mond must have seen the possibilities unfolding before him at Brunner Mond & Company now that Sir John Brunner was dead. In any event, the Prime Minister succumbed. He owed Mond a great deal and by way of inducement, he offered him the next big office that came into his hands, that of Minister of Health.

It was certainly an appointment which excited Mond and it was, perhaps, the only one, other than Chancellor of the Exchequer, that would have deflected him from returning to private industry. Regrettably for Mond, it was a short-lived appointment. He had barely been a year at his new post when Lloyd George called a General Election which saw the Liberals routed and the Tories sweep to Westminster with Bonar Law at their head, a tired and sick man soon to be replaced by Stanley Baldwin. The Socialists, upon whom all Mond's bitterness was concentrated at this time, were in formidable Opposition while the old Liberals sat in the shadows. Mond managed to hold on to his Swansea seat, but as a backbencher he seemed so out of place. He was an unrelenting critic of Socialism and his bitterness made him, and therefore Brunner Mond & Company, the butt of many savage attacks by Labour's Philip Snowden who insisted that his party did not propose revolution, or confiscation, but simply a desire to remove the capitalist from industry, men like Sir Alfred Mond. Yet what Mond failed to perceive was that the electorate was embracing Socialism and like many of his colleagues, including Churchill, he was swept away in the historic General Election of 1923 that soon saw Ramsay MacDonald become Prime Minister of Britain's first Labour Government. It was a severe shock to Mond and though he staggered on to return at a by-election in the Welsh market town of Camarthen, he was out of place and finished. His political star had waned, for Camarthen was an agricultural seat and, despite all his bluster, 'Veils for the Veltch', it hardly seemed a fitting finale for one such as he.

Like the champion boxer refusing to gracefully accept retirement, he was climbing into the ring for one fight too many and the Welsh farming folk were just as suspicious of his motives as had been the electors of Chester twenty years earlier. Nothing was left to chance and two-hundred Liberal cars were said to have ferried voters to the polls to ensure Mond's victory and his return to Westminster from where he pledged to expel the Socialists. The more earthy problems of the Camarthen farmers were quickly forgotten.

Whilst out of office, prior to the by-election, he had sailed away from Britain for two months, to visit his friend, the Viceroy of India, Lord Reading (Rufus Isaacs), and during the long journey he began to map out a new course for himself. Politics might still, briefly, attract him, but it was to industry that he was ready to turn as the launchpad for his radicalism and where better to use his vast influence, power and wealth, to practise his political doctrine, of a strong single party, than at the head of Brunner Mond & Company?

The Daily Graphic

Sir Alfred Mond

Benevolent seems just the word to describe him as he rises - now, unhappily for him, from a back-bench below the Opposition gangway. He does not pretend to be an orator. He just stands up, beams infectiously through his glasses, sticks one thumb in the armhole of his waistcoat, holds a little pocket-book in his other hand, and then proceeds to 'chat' for half an hour, in rather thick tones. But what a 'chat' it usually is !

On economic and industrial questions he is like a human concentrate of all the reference works that were ever written. He likes to make startling assertions, to goad his opponents into the incautious interruption of a challenge. And then, like the falling of a sledge-hammer, comes the production of the devastating fact that has been cuddled up his sleeve in readiness for the appropriate moment. His generously proportioned form, clad in the conventional morning coat and striped cashmere trousers, reminds one irresistibly of the other, lesser commercial men seen standing outside a shop-door and appraising the street's supply of customers.

His glasses balance themselves with complete safety on the bridge of a nose which offers ample accommodation. A great black moustache flows evenly down either side of a mobile and rather impressive mouth. A carnation, accompanied by its spiked leaves, makes a sprightly show of colour in his button-hole.

'Mr Speaker', he begins, and in a moment the House has settled down to wait for the good things which are sure to come. He smiles, and smiles, and smiles. Even when, as is sometimes the case, the laugh is turned against him, the smile continues. His utter imperturbability is amazing.

CHAPTER FIVE
ETHEL BRUNNER - THE AUTHOR

From the lofty heights of Belmont Hall, the Brunners, 'Mr & Mrs Roscoe', gazed over the belching smoke stacks of their sprawling works to a new dawn. The sufferings of the Great War had given way to a world at peace and thousands were home to share in Brunner Mond's international reputation and prosperity. Rich and powerful, master of all he surveyed, Roscoe Brunner was the amiable, patriarchal head of this great concern. He served on this body or that organisation, chaired one committee or another and, to most everyone who ever came into contact with him, he was an affable English gentleman devoted to his workforce, to his father's company and to the town and people of Northwich. He was also, according to the local newspaper, very much in the mould of his father, Sir John:

> He possesses an immensely sanguine temperament and always takes an optimistic view of affairs. His deep voice and his resounding laugh reveal a zest and a joy for life; he is carefree, cheerful, detached from the disagreeable and the ambitious; he has an adored and beautiful wife, worshipped and adoring children...

As for Ethel Brunner, she remained something of a puzzle. Her charity work in the district was legendary, but then with so much wealth and opportunity she was able to indulge in whatever she pleased. There were those who looked upon her as a woman of marked social and artistic gifts, an accomplished singer, a sculptor and a collector of fine arts, but others would point to her impulsiveness and her unpredictability which could so quickly, and violently, swing from the sublimely generous to the absurdly malevolent.

In one instance she would richly reward a servant and, in another, truculently dismiss the entire household staff, a situation which often prevailed upon Roscoe Brunner's alacrity to restore dignity and calm. Ethel Brunner's outpourings of temper were well known amongst the servants and her husband was often the butt of her sometimes uncontrollable raging. One story is told of how, in a fit of anger, she ordered the chauffeur to set fire to Roscoe's brand new car, simply because he had not consulted her before purchasing it. When the chauffeur refused to carry out her orders, she dismissed him!

Below stairs, there were frequent whispers that Roscoe Brunner frequently found solace elsewhere, but if he did then the intimate details certainly never reached the ears of his wife. Of marriage, Ethel Brunner said: 'From closest observation, the one conclusion I've been led to is that the one sphere in which a woman cannot possibly live her own life is that of marriage. She has to obliterate herself entirely.'

Everyone who knew the Brunners, depending of course upon their own relationship with them, had a differing view of Ethel Brunner and though she may have turned to writing out of sheer boredom, it is only as an author that she positively reveals anything of her inner self.

She actually penned four novels between 1916 and 1924, and though all rather quixotic and short on substance, they were reasonably popular in their day. It is within the context of subsequent tragic events that they afford a fascinating insight into her own character.

The heroine of her novels was Celia and there can be no doubt that Celia was Ethel as she perceived herself or, at the very least, as the person she desired to be, though friends and acquaintances reading the novels at the time might not necessarily have recognised an alter ego at work. Had she lived longer, Ethel might perhaps have widened her horizons and the scope of a her talent, but then she was neither driven by need, nor ideals, for her work was simply borne out of the same self-indulgence that so often characterised her life.

Her novels commenced with a slim volume of 150 pages 'Celia and Her Friends', followed in 1917 by 'The Elopement', described as 'a novel in drama form', and in 1919, by 'Celia Once Again' in which Celia and her devoted admirer, Peter Blenerhasset, take in a Continental tour and describe the people they meet. Ethel's final novel, and apparently her best work although, said one critic, devoid of hardly any storyline, was 'Celia's Fantastic Voyage'. In this she discussed at great length a variety of more or less important topics relating to social reform and the analysis of industrial and political motive.

Ethel's major characters appear in all four books and were clearly sculpted from the Brunner and Mond families and those immediately around her. There was Stalybrass, surely her father-in-law's old partner, Ludwig Mond: '...the strident and really unreasonable Labor (sic) Leader whose truculent, trestle-legs planted so obstinately on what he constantly and loudly referred to as free soil.' He was the 'barbaric, over honest, over earnest, uncompromising figure who dismissed things; things that should not be dismissed. And what he did not dismiss he demolished'.

Then there was a former 'Government Minister' overshadowed by the powerful industrialist, Lord Tyneforth. The ex-Minister was almost certainly fashioned upon Sir Alfred Mond, whilst Lord Tyneforth was, undoubtedly, Sir John Brunner of whom Ethel Brunner was a great admirer, in all accept one thing; his refusal to accept a peerage which would have been an impressive adjunct to further her own status. Through Celia and Lord Tyneforth, she was at least able to rectify the error of Sir John's ways, for Lord Everton he may not have become in his lifetime, but Lord Tyneforth he became in her novels. It was also through Lord Tyneforth that Ethel narrated the rise of Brunner Mond & Company with the nightmare and doubts of those early years. She wrote though Lord Tyneforth:

> I well remember the late Autumn of 1878. That was a year for me. It was a rare cold, clammy, dreary and depressing season, that one when I signed the papers purchasing the estate of Millington in the County of Dampshire to build our works on, with Millington Old Hall and Millington New Hall included. For there were two great old mansions there, an old one and a new, bang up, one against the other. The one old and low and rambling, Elizabethan black and white, the other enormous and stately in stone... It was do or die, sink or swim - and there's plenty of water here for both purposes.

It was for the water - and other things of course - we bought it, but principally for the water. Water for the process and water for the freight. On that day in the Autumn of '78 we were perished with cold and frightened well nigh out of our senses at what we were going to do. The solicitors for the Letchmeres did not seem very impressed by me. They didn't like the deal. Knew what it was for, and very naturally did-n't fancy the poor old spot being desecrated by chimneys, coke ovens and blast furnaces and what they knew we meant to do besides. The disappointment, the heartaches, the bad debts, the loads we carried with us day in day out. Our place nearly closed time after time. Every single Saturday that we paid our men for years was a day of crisis for us.

Old Sir John and Ludwig Mond had literally sweat blood in those cold, clammy days of the 1870s and it was hardly surprising that Roscoe and Ethel Brunner were later to feel such bitter resentment when they saw the company slipping away, to be swallowed up in the great crucible of the Imperial Chemicals Industry merger. Roscoe Brunner may not have endured the hardships of his father, but he had inherited from him the trust and the ideals of those early days and he alone of the two families had been left to drive the business ever onward, to success and prosperity.

In Ethel Brunner's novels, her husband was plainly Sir Timothy Strutt, whom she described as 'an admirable pendant to his wife who had the strangest forces of all about him - and the one that defies analysis the most completely.' He possessed, she wrote, '...the absolute expectation and certitude of obtaining first class service and attention for everyone. There was about him the suggestion of an enormous expectation of recognition of himself and his wants or ideas from peo-ple - whose employees served him very anxiously and very efficient-ly. I believe that it would not have been easy for any man coming in contact with him, not to do the best he could whatever it was he was doing'.

As to Celia, she was described as a 'dainty and delightful hostess who was fortunate to possess an exceptionally large circle of witty and amusing friends; one who was so fascinating and so pretty that when men looked at her they got a queer sort of tightening in their chest …Celia, the charming lady, had a great deal of money, through no fault of her own. In fact she was able to spend as much as she liked without bothering her head as to whether she could afford it or not. But she is not selfish and her great idea is that some day, sometime, she'll be able to do something large and productive towards helping the world along and that the money will come in very useful when she finds her opening'.

In her latter years, Ethel Brunner actually discovered the very opening for the philanthropy which she so desired through Celia and she devoted much of herself to financially supporting the famous Dr Spahlinger, of Geneva, who was working on finding a cure for tuberculosis.

Celia's devoted admirer was always Peter Blenerhasset through whom Ethel narrated her novels, but he was something of a mystery to the heroine and she was strangely undecided about him. The redoubtable Peter is also a mystery in the autobiographical sense of Ethel's novels. As all other major characters seem to have a place in reality, was she herself having an affair behind Roscoe's back, or was she merely using Peter as a male vehicle to indulge her own vanity? If she did have an extra-marital suitor, and the only existing references in this direction are to a mysterious London solicitor by the name of 'Pierre', then she was far too circumspect to allow the matter to become public and to their circle of friends she always appeared the perfect wife.

As the 'Lady Bountiful of Belmont Hall', Ethel was called upon to open bazaars and garden parties, to distribute school prizes, to lecture on housewifery and to serve on committees of numerous local charities. But as the wife of a staunch Liberal family, whose own father stood for the cause in Warrington, it was remarkable that she steadfastly supported the Conservative Party. Sir John and Jack Brunner may have been in the House of Commons, sitting as Liberals, and her husband their most ardent supporter, but Ethel never waivered from the Conservatives as she organised fetes, soirees, masked balls, dinners and concerts to raise funds. Like Sir Alfred Mond, she despised the march of Socialism, as she put it, 'the New Order ...the Extremist party with comic opera economics' and, to her, Conservatism was the only means of its defeat.

She was certainly not well liked within the Brunner and Mond families and only Sir John saw fit to humour her impetuousness, if only for the sake of his grandchildren, Shelagh, Patrick and Anthony. How poor Roscoe Brunner viewed his wife's determination to support the Conservatives, and what embarrassment he must have suffered, is not documented, but years later he too joined the ranks. Any notion of Roscoe himself entering politics was always instantly dismissed with a scornful laugh. Not for him the complications and futilities of such a career. Almost born to a fortune, the head of a major British company, he had not a moment to spare for things outside his family, his business and Cheshire. He simply had no ambition to be anyone else. He was himself, unenvious of any man; happy with his position as a prominent industrialist.

There is no doubt that Ethel Brunner was a calculating woman and to ensure that she kept abreast of her husband's business affairs, she would resort to her own wily feminine ways to engineer and influence the decision-making, to further her husband's career which so reflected her own standing within society. Indeed, in the Foreword to 'Celia's Fantastic Voyage' one particular passage came to reverberate throughout the inquiry into the Roehampton tragedy:

'Celia was so obsessed with the idea that she would be able to manoeuvre things into happening that she never did any single thing in the whole of her life without a motive. Whether it was to order a new hat, cross a room, sit down on a chair, or take a cup of tea with an uninteresting woman, she always had a motive. She said herself that she never made a friend or shook hands with a person except with a view to using them for something. She lived an altogether very involved and intricate life, densely surrounded by motives...'

So from the splendour of Belmont Hall, Ethel Brunner arranged her lavish dinner parties and in the grounds Roscoe Brunner would regale his most trusted colleagues, J.H.Gold and J.G.Nicholson who made up what came to be known as a Brunner Mond management triumvirate. Tennis and croquet over, the trio would relax to plot the next move in Brunner Mond's fortunes and always by Roscoe Brunner's side was his wife, who had every reason to encourage the triumvirate, because through it she knew more of the company's business dealings than the rest of the directors put together, and almost as much as her husband and his privileged colleagues. With the exception of Sir Alfred Mond's cousin Emile, who served as the politician's 'eyes and ears' on the Brunner Mond board, the directors were content that this informal committee should enjoy their freedom of action and the triumvirate seldom felt obliged to keep their colleagues informed of what they were doing.

Ethel Brunner relished the situation, for though women were fervently demanding their rights, they had hardly begun to knock on the door of the male-dominated bastions of industry. Not for her the

Belmont Hall, Cheshire, the home of Roscoe and Ethel Brunner.

Suffrage movement; there had been no need to chain herself to Buckingham Palace, nor to join the disciples of Mrs Emmeline Pankhurst. There were few obstacles before her and since she could not invade the strict preserves of the Brunner Mond boardroom, she manoeuvred the boardroom to Belmont Hall. She influenced, some might say interfered, but always with her husband's blessing and her furthest thought was to undermine his and, therefore, her own position.

Brunner Mond's standing was immense, both as a hugely successful international business and as a model employer, offering good pay, holidays, shorter hours, housing and a health service. In return, the company expected complete authority over their men at work and a strong influence outside as well.

Indeed, when Sir John Brunner finally passed on the company chairmanship to Roscoe it represented to Ethel Brunner, for the time being at least, the efflorescence of all she had ever dreamed. However, within little over twelve months of formally relinquishing the reins of power, Sir John was dead. In failing health, he had spent his latter years as a widower at his mansion in Chertsey, Surrey, a stone's throw from the home of the former Prime Minister, Lloyd George. Sir John had become so disillusioned with the squabbling and bickering within the Liberal Party that on the occasion of the 1919 General Election, he financially supported the local Labour Party.

Roscoe Brunner had acted as chairman of Brunner Mond in everything but name for the best part of fifteen years and his selflessness, integrity and mastery of profession ensured the complete confidence of all those around him. With his able lieutenants, Gold and Nicholson, he had successfully steered the company through the turbulence of the First World War and was ready to chart a vibrant new peacetime course. The war had accelerated chemical technology and as Brunner Mond's profits soared during the first five years of his stewardship, his position was assured, or so it seemed.

Few had reason to complain and when, following the death of Sir John, at the age of eighty, they built a bronze statue to the old founder, in the pose of him addressing a public meeting and to stand fittingly at Winnington, near to the statue of his partner Ludwig Mond, it was with absolute certitude that Roscoe Brunner looked to the future. As Minister of Health, Sir Alfred Mond formally unveiled the statue and, with Roscoe Brunner, he officiated at week-long celebrations to mark the company's Golden Jubilee. During the formal proceedings, Mr J.A.Cowley, the local town clerk of Northwich, said of Roscoe Brunner:

> We honour him for the great position he holds - a worthy son of a worthy sire. Some achieve greatness, some have greatness thrust upon them. Although Mr Roscoe Brunner was the son of his father, he has attained the position of chairman by sheer merit. And we who depend so much upon Brunner Mond and Company for our well-being consider that the destinies of this great company are in safe hands. There is a noble band of workers, and young and energetic though they may be, they need a gentleman to lead them, and in Mr Roscoe Brunner the great administrators of this firm can have have no better leader.

One who certainly would not have agreed was Sir Alfred Mond who served notice of his imperialistic intentions. He said he wanted a great business of world-wide reputation, a sort of legitimate pride, not only to the immediate neighbourhood, but to the country, to make it greatly more respected, more powerful throughout the markets of the Empire, throughout the markets of the world.

Unveiling of Sir John Brunner's statue at Winnington.

Sir Alfred Mond's home, Melchet Court in Hampshire.

CHAPTER SIX
ROYAL WEDDING

A single topic above all others provoked fierce argument at Belmont Hall throughout the early years of the 1920s and it centred upon Roscoe Brunner's refusal to consider a permanent move to London and the Cavendish Square head offices of Brunner Mond. To Ethel Brunner, London was a natural development and the rightful place for the head of an international business which had long since outgrown its parochial status. Her arguments were certainly valid, but no amount of cajoling, or brow-beating, could ever change her husband's opinion and though he had many opportunities to move to the capital, he spurned them all, for to him the very idea was an anathema.

His friends and his public life were in Cheshire and, besides, whenever he needed to be in London, there was always a company apartment at his disposal, in Cavendish Square. He considered his was a simple, but fulfilling life, founded on regularity and routine. On the other hand, his wife yearned for the bright lights of London. For over twenty years she had buried and busied herself in what she said was a 'provincial little town', and she desperately wanted to move into London society where values were no longer necessarily measured in breeding, position or title. The new 'vulgar' industrial upper classes were changing all that.

In one of her 'Celia' novels, Ethel obliquely raises the question of London and she was probably relating Roscoe's view when she wrote:

'I find this business life in London doesn't bring out too successfully the good we have in us, if by chance there is any. City life feeds the passions and starves the emotions till they very nearly perish away, and the passions get overgrown and big. If it's not one, it's another. Pride, envy, emulation, oh – everything, whilst one's true feelings can't make themselves felt.'

The counter-argument was certainly Ethel's: 'It's an excellent place, if you would give some consideration to your way of life in it. My life is my own, why isn't yours yours?'

Whatever the merits, or otherwise, of London, Roscoe and Ethel Brunner were in agreement that it was the place to find a husband for their daughter, Shelagh who, at twenty-six, was approaching spinsterhood in the whirl-wind, self-indulgent world of the 1920s. Hardly considered a woman of great beauty, Shelagh had enjoyed the finest education and finishing that money could buy and, with her father's wealth behind her, she was not short of suitors, but none matched the expectations of Ethel who was fearful that her daughter was more likely to 'walk to the altar in her riding habit'.

Shelagh Brunner.

As mothers do, Ethel's anxiety increased when she attended the marriage of Roscoe's niece, Joyce Morgan Brunner, the daughter of Jack Brunner, to William Worsley, the son of Sir William Worsley, bart. It was a grand occasion and prominent reports of the wedding in the London society pages served only to rouse Ethel's determination to find Shelagh a fitting husband, of the highest social standing possible.

(It is interesting to note that Joyce and William Worsley's own daughter, Katherine Lucy Mary Worsley, the great grand-daughter of Sir John Brunner, married King George V's grandson in 1961 and so became the present Duchess of Kent.)

Ethel Brunner must also have cast an envious glance at Sir Alfred Mond's family for, in terms of connections, his children mixed freely with some of the rich and fashionable socialites of the day, sponsored as they were by their father's political standing and, to an extent, his German ancestry. One of Mond's daughters, Eva had already married the son of Lord Reading, and in their turn, her sisters, Mary and Nora, were close friends of Edwina Ashley and 'Dickie' Battenberg, and many others from the families of the Cassels, Hirschts, Wernhers and

Teks, some of whom were cousins to the Royal Family. Indeed at the height of the anti-German clamour in 1914, King George had agreed that those of his cousins who were British citizens should be Anglicised as, of course, by virtue of Queen Victoria's marriage to Prince Albert, he was himself a Saxe-Coburg-Gotha. The entirely spurious House of 'Windsor' was established and the Battenbergs were retitled as the Marquess and Marchionesse of Milford Haven, with 'Dickie' Battenberg becoming Lord Louis Mountbatten. Others in this circle of Mond family acquaintances included Freda Dudley Ward, the close friend of the Prince of Wales. It was fair to say that Shelagh Brunner, for all her fine education and finishing, was not privy to such exalted company and so Ethel resorted to the best alternative: a marriage through the famous London 'arrangers', Countess Mazarine and Ferrard, of Lancaster Gate. Shelagh possessed, as it were, the dowry and Ethel was prepared to trawl Europe to find someone to make them all turn their heads.

The arranged suitors came and went, all vetted and rejected by Ethel as inappropriate for one reason or another, until the arrival upon the scene of one of the most eligible of European bachelors, at least in title and prestige. He was Prince Ferdinand Andreas de Liechtenstein, the nephew of the Crown Prince of Liechtenstein, the tiny Alpine state nestled alongside Lake Constance and set between Germany and Switzerland. The Prince's connections and his social standing were immense. His father had been a personal friend of both King Edward VII and King George V; his aunt, Princess Marriza, was the accepted leader of Viennese society and his great uncle, Count Andrassy, was a former Prime Minister of Hungary.

Ethel Brunner was overjoyed and she was quite prepared to ignore what others might believe, that the Prince, though well known in European diplomatic and financial circles, was a penniless philanderer. Shelagh was literally swept off her feet when her knight in shining armour dashed across Europe to obtain sanction and the passing of a special Bill in the Liechtenstein Parliament, enabling him to claim his bride as the first member of the Liechtenstein Royal Family to marry a commoner.

This was the moment Ethel Brunner had been longing for. She had always harboured a tendency to be outrageously ostentatious in the muck and manure set of Cheshire. It was part of her make-up and now she could turn her self-perceived sophistication and exquisite taste into creating the society wedding of the year.

What she conjured up was the most incredible spectacle, the like of which had seldom been seen outside the most aristocratic circles of England. She threw dinner party upon dinner party to extol the merits of her daughter's impending marriage to Prince Ferdinand. It was the greatest social coup she could have engineered and as the wedding guest list soared into hundreds, it became more akin to a list from Who's Who?. There were to be Princes, Princesses, Counts and Countesses, Barons and Viscounts and scores of legations from the countries of Europe.

Not for Ethel was this to be a parochial, or even a county wedding and, as it was necessary for Shelagh to adopt the Liechtenstein Royal Family's Catholicism, the splendour of London's Brompton Oratory was chosen as the setting, in keeping with so many of the finest society weddings of the day. The great ceremony in St Wilfrid's Chapel took place on Wednesday January 14th, 1925, and Ethel went far beyond the extremes to turn it into a fantasy wedding with which to publicly impress London society. It was to be Shelagh's wedding, but Ethel's crowning glory.

A large crowd gathered outside to witness the occasion and scores of invited guests were unable to get further than the church door, for not even Brompton Oratory was sufficiently large to accommodate Ethel's guest list. The bridesmaids, eight in all, including the Princess Gabrielle of Liechtenstein, were attired in gowns of gold lace, embroidered with rubies, all topped with head-dresses in gold tissue. The best man, Count Terence Erdody, was in spectacular Hungarian nobleman's uniform of the 15th century, rich purple, velvet and silver, and the scene was described as one of 'unsurpassing splendour'; the great white marble pilasters and shining gilded cornices of the sanctuary adding to a magnificent collage of colour, all complemented by the mass choirs and music of the Brompton Oratory.

On Roscoe Brunner's arm came the bride, 'unbelievably stunning,' reported the newspapers, in a robe of gold lace, her long full train lined with gold tissue and a head-dress topped with a gold coronet. At the conclusion of the marriage rite, the bride and bridegroom knelt whilst the priest read aloud a telegram from the Pope: 'The Holy Father imparts his Apostolic Benediction to his dear children, Ferdinand de Liechtenstein and Shelagh Brunner, on their marriage.'

Afterwards, the guests retired to Claridges for a formal reception which, to a young reporter from Shelagh's home town of Northwich, was on a 'scale of sumptuousness rather easier to imagine than describe'. The wedding party, he noted, took over a suite of three state rooms and, with the famous Claridges' orchestra playing amidst the palms and flowering shrubs, it was altogether a brilliant scene, '...the happy bridegroom with his radiant bride, the throng of distinguished guests in their charming frocks, gleaming jewels and magnificent furs'.

Interviewed by the press, the dashing Prince, fluent in English, German, French and Italian, spoke lovingly of his wife. She was a fine horsewoman and tennis player and he would be introducing her to his own speciality, that of mountaineering. He hoped too that she would soon learn to speak German, the language most commonly used by Liechtenstein's tiny population of just 10,000. His uncle, the Crown Prince Johann II, owned vast estates across Europe and it was intended, said the Prince, that he would be given management responsibility for some of these.

How Ethel enjoyed and savoured the occasion, the attention of the press and the limelight which she had so craved, whilst Roscoe was happy to play the father's role, delighted with his daughter's good fortune and content to see his wife aspire to a new exalted position in society. It was all, as was Ethel's way, a bit over the top and it brought its nemesis, for hardly had the euphoria of Shelagh's wedding subsided than the storm clouds began to gather for a shattering climax to one of the biggest corporate quarrels in the annals of British business. The consequences were to be enormous, hastening the demise of Brunner Mond & Company, the birth of Imperial Chemical Industries and the deaths of Roscoe and Ethel Brunner.

CHAPTER SEVEN
NEW HORIZONS

With the precarious Welsh seat of Camarthen in his pocket, Sir Alfred Mond had continued his flirtation with politics and often he would head the depleted Liberal forces in the House of Commons, but it was without the passion and self belief that had carried him so far. However, when yet another General Election was called in, he exercised decisive influence on the fate of 20th century British politics.

Lloyd George had been forced to hastily curtail a trip to America and when the Mauritania docked at Southampton, Mond was there heading a Liberal deputation imploring him to fight for the cause of Free Trade. Churchill also intervened, sending a hand-delivered letter, begging his leader to side with Mond rather than declare support for some form of Empire Protectionism. It is a matter of history that Lloyd George took their advice and the Liberals were heavily defeated, never since to rise as a governing power in Britain. One of the great ironies was that, later, Mond and Churchill both joined the Conservative Party.

Mond's rift with the Liberals occurred when he became fiercely opposed to plans by Lloyd George to introduce a sweeping land policy, a form of State ownership. Mond complained that it was a 'blundering attempt at bureaucratic socialism' that stood for everything he despised, although neither the press nor the public were altogether sure of his motives. The newspapers said he was a clever and ambitious man and many thought it was clear that he was engaged in a conflict with Lloyd George, a personal conflict in which he was aspiring to fill the Liberal leader's position himself. Mond's biographer dismisses the charge, reasoning that if he had one profound regret, it was his failure, above all else, to become Chancellor of the Exchequer.

Of Lloyd George, Mond said, scathingly: 'The hinderance to his greatness is that he cannot bear a man who has the instincts and code of a gentleman near him for long. It gives him an inferiority complex.' Of Asquith, Lord Oxford, Mond said he was 'barred from true greatness by indecision and the lack of any sense of adventure' and as for Stanley Baldwin, he often confused his responsibilities with those of the Archbishop of Canterbury. 'I am not as simple as I seem,' Baldwin had once protested to Mond. But Mond said, bitingly, he was quite certain that Mr Baldwin would never convince the British public that this was true.

Finally, on January 23rd, 1926, with half-hearted Liberal support for Lloyd George's land policy, Mond submitted his resignation from the Liberal Party. He wrote to Asquith:

> The position of the Liberal Party has been steadily drifting from bad to worse. The unity which we have striven for, and which I did my best to promote, has in fact never been achieved and all efforts to revive and reorganise the Liberal forces have been rendered hopeless by the introduction by Mr Lloyd George of a Land Policy which has produced a new, profound cleavage and embarrassment in the Liberal ranks... the only course for me to take is to sever my lifelong connection with the Liberal Party and... join the party with whom I feel I can most usefully co-operate, the Conservative Party. That such a step is a big break and wrench for me...

Lloyd George was at his home in Chertsey when suddenly, without warning, normal programmes on the wireless were interrupted to announce Sir Alfred Mond's resignation. Lloyd George was furious and when the newspapers began calling for his comments, he said that 'like another notorious member of his race, Alfred Mond had gone to his own place'. Mond's biographer noted that Lloyd George had turned to the Acts of the Apostles to find his venomous metaphor to liken Mond to Judas Iscariot, although in his anger he had failed to realise the handsome compliment he had paid to himself.

Looking back years later, Lloyd George declared: 'What made me angry on the night, when the news came over the wireless, was because he had sent his letter to Asquith and not to me. Asquith was not the leader of the party in the House. I was bitter and I hit out. It was not because Mond had changed. Winston Churchill changed his party and I never quarrelled with him. It was discourteous and ungrateful of Mond to announce his decision without writing to me - it was I who twice gave Mond office in my Government, against definite opposition from everybody except Bonar Law. And he wrote to Asquith ! Asquith who had snubbed him; Asquith who had never even given him an under-secretaryship.'

The dye was cast and Mond knew in his heart that his political career was effectively over from the moment he dispatched his letter of resignation to Asquith, for whatever his talents of statesmanship, he was not a Winston Churchill to be welcomed like a prodigal son to the bosom of an Opposition Party. Indeed, the everyday rutting season of politics was in full cry when the outcast Mond took his new place in the House of Commons. The Liberals howled their disapproval, the Conservatives were cold and mistrusting of their former enemy and Lloyd George wondered what twenty pieces of silver might buy. Sir Alfred Mond had become a political embarrassment. He had nailed his colours to the mast, but he point-blank refused to recontest his Camarthen seat as a Conservative and Stanley Baldwin, the British Prime Minister, was left to offer an unwelcoming hand of friendship, though it mattered little to Mond for few men hold office of state without possessing an immense ego and, besides, he had already resolved to seize power elsewhere, in his own inimitable style, unfettered by politics or the electorate.

Upon leaving the main arena of politics to return to business he said: 'I have nothing more to gain or seek in the political field. I have held office in State at the time of the country's greatest crisis. I have had as much political honour as any man may require, and I would gladly leave the work to younger hands.'

In a formal memorial publication, following Mond's death in 1930, I.C.I. went further to explain his reasoning:

Freed from office, industry and the immense schemes of industrial reorganisation that had already shaped themselves in his mind, instantly claimed him; and his severance from his former political association meant little more to him than the dropping of an investment that had lost its efficacy and the seizure of one that still seemed sound and serviceable. The project he was meditating went beyond all party lines.

Meanwhile, the acrimony between Brunner Mond and the soap manufacturers Lever Brothers had been fermenting since the end of the war and within months of Sir Alfred Mond reclaiming his seat on the board of the chemical company, matters began veering towards a devastating conclusion.

Hesketh Lever, the head of the soap giants, discovered that Brunner Mond, despite an undertaking not to sell alkali more cheaply to any other soapmaker, had in fact been doing just that. He was bitterly angry at the chemical company's duplicity and the consequences at Brunner Mond were dire. Roscoe Brunner's lieutenant, J.H.Gold, resigned and, in a curiously abrupt termination of a role which he had filled for so many years, Brunner was forced to relinquish the chairmanship, although out of deference to the Brunner family, he was allowed to retain his directorship. The official reason for his sudden resignation was 'ill health' and yet within weeks of him stepping down, he was anticipating an exciting new challenge with the company, not in Cheshire, but in London, the one place to which he had always been so resolutely opposed.

So it was that Sir Alfred Mond accepted the chairmanship of Brunner Mond & Company. He continued to represent the Camarthen seat in the House of Commons, but his new mission was to become an industrial statesman as he viewed, with a mixture of admiration and apprehension, the huge manufacturing capabilities of the United States and Germany.

Exasperated by caution and convention, he demanded a vigorous new approach through 'rationalisation', a term which he is generally accredited as being the first to use and whose very mention still furrows the brow of workers the world over. To Mond, it was a race for supremacy and from the minute he succeeded to the chairmanship of Brunner Mond he tabled ideas of grand imperial design, bold, far-seeing and utterly ruthless, contrasting markedly with the paternal hand of the Brunners. Absolute power had continually eluded the autocrat Mond in politics, but in industry he was free to pursue his goals with relative impunity. As far as he was concerned, big brains and ruthless efficiency were required, not high-mindedness and persuasive mediocrity.

He certainly considered himself morally and intellectually superior to most of his fellow men and anyone who raised the slightest objection to his plans was destined to be excluded, or crushed, as he simply swept his colleagues along with him. Only his son, Henry, was ever permitted to become a true confidante.

Referring to his own father, Mond noted: 'I was reading a letter not very long ago, which my father wrote when he was a very young man. He said he would not seek success, he would compel it...'

This, with all the astuteness he had honed as a Parliamentarian, came to be his own business maxim and, in spite of the prevailing discord in Britain, he began propelling Brunner Mond towards extraordinary, and previously unthinkable, new horizons.

In 1926, the year of the General Strike, Britain was a nation of uncertainty, of restlessness, of political turmoil and of industrial strife. It had not become a land fit for heroes as the politicians had promised and the soldiers were home, harassed people, with their leaders trapped in a failing economy, unemployment and social distress its anathema.

The General Strike, a trial of strength between the militants of Trade Unionsim and the State, was called in support of a national coal stoppage, caused partly by the reopening of the German mines and partly by the return of the gold standard, hastened by the Chancellor of the Exchequer, Winston Churchill. To compensate for lost trade and profits, the coal owners made a shattering ultimatum – if Britain's miners wanted to keep their jobs, they would have to take cuts in pay and work longer hours. The miners responded with the famous slogan... 'Not a penny off the pay, not a minute on the day'.

It was stalemate and Government efforts to reconcile the factions failed and on May 1st, 1926, the coal owners closed the pits. Two days later, Britain came to a complete standstill in what was an unprecedented crisis as hundreds of thousands of workers responded to the call to leave their jobs and forfeit their pay in support of the miners. When the General Strike eventually collapsed, the miners were left to stand alone for another six months before agreeing to return for longer hours and lower wages.

Many eminent politicians and industrial leaders had their say on the best way to formulate a lasting peace, but few did so more forcibly than Sir Alfred Mond who regularly monopolised The Times' letters column to expound upon his theories and to cite Germany as a shining beacon of hope. Needless to say, it was not the most diplomatic argument that he had ever presented and the miners responded by angrily raking over the embers of his German ancestry and his patriotism.

It was in the midst of this turmoil that Mond set about forging Imperial Chemical Industries with Sir Harry McGowan, the Chairman and Managing Director of Nobel Industries Ltd, the British arm of the international explosives industry, founded by Alfred Nobel, the inventor of dynamite and the instigator of the Nobel Peace Prize. McGowan was the ultimate self-made man, a flamboyant bon viveur who had risen from an obscure Glaswegian background.

At the outset, that is to say during the first half of 1926, Mond was not greatly impressed with the idea of forming a 'big British combine', as McGowan put it. He was pre-occupied with oil-from-coal and he wanted to exploit the expertise of Germany's IG Farben dyes and chemical group, a world leader in the field. What he proposed therefore was for Brunner Mond to join forces in a worldwide consortium with IG Farben and the American Chemical & Dye Corporation, operating under a flag of convenience, a holding company based in London with an authorized capital of around £25 million.

The Germans were in full agreement and Mond hastened to New

York where he was just about to formally develop talks when McGowan appeared on the scene, anxious to protect the interests of Nobel Industries. McGowan was enormously energetic and imaginative in his business dealings and when he met Mond over the lunch table he began at once strongly pressing for a merger of the four leading British chemical companies, hinting that if Mond did not agree, Nobel Industries would turn its own attentions to linking up with the IG Farben Group.

In the end Mond relented and on October 6th, 1926, the RMS Aquitania sailed sedately out of New York bound for Southampton. One of the most handsome liners afloat, she was like some great Georgian mansion, oozing luxury, grandeur and opulence, and with a passenger list tending towards the pages of Burke or Debrett. By day, Harris tweed, Chanel jerseys, indolent conversation and energetic sport; by night, a sudden increase in tempo, a blaze of jewels, the gleam of ivory shoulders, the formality brilliance with which aristocratic English life was so perfectly at ease.

On board were Mond and McGowan and here, amidst the grand setting of the Palm Courts, the Palladian lounge and the Louis XlV dining room, these two autocratic captains of industry formulated their Magna Carta, their own Bill of Rights, what came to be known as the 'Aquitania Agreement', from which spawned one of the most far-reaching and profound mergers in British industrial history, the creation of Imperial Chemical Industries.

Sketched on four sheets of Cunard Line notepaper, the 'Aquitania Agreement' came to be the blueprint for Sir Alfred Mond and Sir Harry McGowan's masterplan as they set themselves weeks to fashion their new empire. Throughout the six-day voyage they worked, night and day, to put the pieces into place, and nor did they rest on the seventh day, for within hours of disembarking at Southampton, they were negotiating to take over the entire British chemical industry, lock, stock and barrel.

They were not men to immerse themselves in trifling detail and once they had set their minds to a merger, there was only the grand scheme of things to consider. At this stage, shareholders and employees simply did not enter into their calculations. They decided that Mond should be the chairman, with McGowan as president, and together they were to have absolute executive authority for the new business which, as early as the Atlantic crossing, it was agreed they would call Imperial Chemical Industries, a name, which did not meet with the approval of the Registrar of Companies, so prompting Mond, in a fit of outrage, to complain to the President of the Board of Trade who then reversed the decision. 'We are Imperial in aspect and Imperial in name,' he said grandly.

Mond's political frustrations were forgotten. He was fifty-seven and his keenly developed instinct for self-preservation was steering him towards supreme leadership of what was to become an industrial giant. Writing twelve months later to the IG Farben Group, he rather pompously described himself as the 'Head of the Chemical Industry in this country, and the inheritor of the position of promoter of the Chemical Industry from one of its greatest leaders, my late father'.

Working feverishly from an office overlooking Smith Square, in Westminster, Mond and McGowan set about the immense task of preparing their proposals which were to carry the shareholders of the merging companies and exactly one week later, on October 21st, they were ready to make a public announcement which was to cause a sensation in industrial circles. Mond wrote to the press:

> Mergers of interest of such magnitude as have been outlined by the directors of the four chemical and explosives concerns of this country are not merely a question of financial or commercial interest, but have a wider national and Imperial aspect. The formation of a great combination such as IG, the Steel Trust, and similar combinations in Germany and other parts of the Continent, the existence of the great chemical groups... have forced the leaders of the chemical industry in this country to consider the relative position of their individual concerns and the industry as a whole. After very careful consideration, they have come to the conclusion that the time has arrived for the British and Imperial Chemical

industry to endeavour to form equally a united front. It is not intended to destroy the identity of the autonomy of the individed units composing the new company to be formed. The Boards of these companies will continue to operate the respective industries with which they are most intimately associated.The Board of the new company will form a supervising and connecting link in finance and policy, in exchange of knowledge and information, and will enable the British chemical industry to deal with similar large groups in other countries on terms of equality, enable them to speak with a united voice, and, instead of leaving it to individual units to make arrangements for the world's competitive conditions as best they can, will give them all the authority and prestige and advantages of a great combination...

Always the politician, saying one thing and doing another, it transpired that Mond, in fact, had no intention of allowing the converging companies any rights whatsoever to control their own destinies and, once he had carried the shareholders, he planned to unfurl his proverbial hidden agenda which amounted to a total abandonment of all individual indentity.

He insisted: 'We are on trial before the eyes of the entire world, and especially of our fellow citizens and of the Empire. We are not merely a body of people carrying on industry in order to make dividends, we are much more; we are the object of universal envy, admiration and criticism, and the capacity of British industrialists and British commercialists and British technicians will be judged by the entire world from the success we make of this merger.'

The 'Royal Wedding'... Shelagh Brunner and Prince Ferdinand Andreas de Liechtenstein.

Sir William Hesketh Lever.

Sir Harry McGowan.

Sir Alfred Mond with Lloyd George.

Jack Brunner.

Henry Mond.

THE CATCH OF THE SEASON.

Mond and Stanley Baldwin.. a cartoon from Punch, February 1926.

"THE DILUVIANS"

From the Cartoon in *Punch* by Bernard Partridge.

Lloyd George : "Give you a tow to Ararat?"
Alfred Mond : "Thank you, I'm all for getting back to the land, but I rather mistrust your craft."

A cartoon from Punch, February 1926 - the caption read: 'Sir Alfred Mond, while expressing his eagerness for agricultural reform, has severely criticised Mr Lloyd George's new Land Scheme.' This was the split that led to Mond quitting the Liberals and returning to the board of Brunner Mond & Co..

CHAPTER EIGHT
INQUEST AND SPECULATION

Disbelief and incredulity swept the vast workforce of Brunner Mond & Company when the mind-numbing news of the deaths of Roscoe and Ethel Brunner began to break in the early days of November 1926 and nowhere was the grief more acutely felt than in Cheshire, the cradle of the great chemical undertaking and the home of 'Mr & Mrs Roscoe'. For over fifty years, Brunner Mond & Company had dominated the life and fortunes of the district and practically every family, in every street for miles around, had at least one member of the household working at the 'Chimic'. There was no rule that jobs went from father to son, no agreement that generation should follow generation, but the lineage continued, unbroken and unyielding. For so long at their head had been Roscoe Brunner whose life had now, suddenly, been cut short... in the most tragic and unimaginable circumstances.

Amongst the thousands who stopped to mourn and remember was a rising young engineer, Jack McCormack who never forgot the dreadful sorrow of that cold November morning.

'At first it was just a rumour, spreading like wildfire from one man to the other, but nobody knew for certain.' he said. 'And then it was confirmed by one of the managers. You cannot imagine the esteem with which Roscoe Brunner was held and his death, in the tragic circumstances outlined to us, was a terrible shock. Whatever had happened during the previous year regarding Mr Roscoe's removal from the chairmanship, he was Brunner Mond and we were all stunned beyond belief. I was a draughtsman with Brunner Mond in the 1920s, originally indentured as an apprentice fitter. I did not, of course, mix in the exalted circles of the Brunner family, but we all knew Roscoe Brunner as a charming man with a quiet demeanour. He was a prominent figurehead and when he gave up his position as chairman of

Brunner Mond we heard that his wife reacted violently, accusing him of cowardice. We all knew that the reason, 'ill-health', was just an excuse. Mrs Brunner, by all accounts, was rather pushy. It was felt at the time that Sir Alfred Mond had conspired against Mr Brunner.'

Officially, the workforce were told only what could be contained in a bland four-line statement pinned to communal noticeboards and from that moment, insisted Jack McCormack, the matter was never again formally mentioned. All that remained, as a mark of respect, was a partial suspension of production at the company's many works on the day of Roscoe and Ethel Brunner's funerals.

'That was it,' bitterly recalled Jack McCormack. 'Mr and Mrs Roscoe were wiped off the face of the earth and they were instantly consigned to history by the company hierachy. Roscoe Brunner's epitaph, for all his efforts and the prosperity he had brought to Brunner Mond, was four miserable lines...'

It was left to the local council to sum up the feelings of Cheshire and Mr J.A.Cowley, the Northwich town clerk, wrote:

> The poignancy of the dreadful happening has stirred the whole district, which has been moved in sympathy with the bereaved children and Sir John Brunner. Mr Roscoe Brunner was a thorough English gentleman. He had the natural English sympathies with all forms of suffering and want, and he was the embodiment of all that was good and uplifting. All who had dealings with him testify to his high character, and Northwich people in particular always entertained a high regard for him. If there was one trait in his character that stood out above all others, it was his kindness of heart. He will be remembered not only as a great employer of labour and a great man in the world of commerce, but as a kindly Christian gentleman, of the noble life he lived and the good work he accomplished. Sir John Brunner, in the great calamity that has befallen him, will find some measure of comfort and solace in the thought that those who knew him best, since the late Mr Brunner had lived amongst them so long, have a depth of sympathy for him which cannot be

expressed in mere words. Mrs Brunner was a woman of great personal charm and undoubted ability, and took a tremendous interest in her husband's welfare and business relations. Those who knew Mrs Brunner best knew her as a kindly lady and one who was prepared to go to any lengths to right a wrong. Her consuming desire to help the consumptive of the country was entirely in keeping with her general character. The council has crossed swords with Mr Brunner as representing his company at times, but of him it can be said with truth that his motive was pure. There was no bitterness - just dogged tenacity of the business mind. We knew him so well that we testify that we have lost a really true friend. We in Northwich will be much poorer by our loss.

The editor of the local newspaper was equally glowing in his praise of Roscoe Brunner, but of Ethel Brunner, he was less than fulsome: 'She was possessed of an attractive personality and a winsome disposition. She was an ideal hostess to the guests at Belmont Hall who were many and varied. She was honourable to a degree, and her generosity was well known...'

They were hardly the words Ethel Brunner would have chosen, but then her strong Conservative views had not always held favour with the editor of a staunch Liberal newspaper.

The national press was awash with speculation following the Green Cottage tragedy and by the following Monday, November 8th, the headlines had become so strident and so sensational that they fuelled the curiosity of a morbid crowd of sightseers who besieged the formal inquest to hear for themselves the story of how such a wealthy and privileged couple had apparently become murderer and victim. The inquest was held in the unlikely setting of Wandsworth Baths and such was the commotion that the Westminster Coroner, Dr. Samuel Ingleby Oddie, ordered that only journalists would be allowed access to observe the proceedings and members of the public were excluded.

The opening witness was Jack Brunner (Sir John Brunner, 2nd Bart.)

who testified that his brother, Roscoe Brunner, was fifty-five years of age and had recently given up his house, Belmont Hall, in Cheshire, and had taken Roehampton Court, near to London, but at the time of his death he was not occupying either residence. He was a director of public companies. His brother's wife, to the best of his belief, was forty-nine, and they were married in 1898. He last saw Roscoe Brunner on October 25th at a board meeting of Brunner Mond & Company, in Cavendish Square. His brother, he said, had been chairman of the company since 1918, but had vacated the chair and had been succeeded by Sir Alfred Mond.

Coroner - The vacating of the chair would be I suppose at the request of the board of directors and for good reason I dare-say?

Sir John Brunner - Yes, it was stated at the annual meeting of the company that it was on account of his poor health.

Coroner - And was there any other reason?

Yes -There were serious business troubles.

Coroner - For which he, as chairman, I take it, had to take responsibility?

Yes, he had to take responsibility.

Coroner - Do you know of your own knowledge whether the giving up of the chairmanship was rather felt by him?

Yes, it was a serious blow to him.

Coroner - Can you tell me when the new board of the new company, which I understand is being formed, was consti-tuted?

The board is not yet constituted - it is only proposed.

Coroner - But tentatively has the board been suggested?

Yes.

Coroner - And a new company formed in which there is a combination of Brunner Mond and other companies? Yes.

Coroner - Was he suggested as a director of this new amal-gamated company or not?

No sir. His name was not among those which were pub-lished.

Coroner - Do you know that it would have been a great disappointment to him?

It was a very severe disappointment to him.

Coroner - At what date did he get this information?

On October 25 at the board meeting I have referred to.

Coroner - Has he written to you since that date upon the subject?

No.

Coroner - You mention his health in your statement. What do you know?

He had been very ill for quite two years.

Coroner - Do you know the nature of his illness?

He had a very serious attack of shingles. A very nervous disease; very painful.

Coroner - You have never heard of him speak of suicide?

No, never.

Coroner - Did you know he had a revolver?

No, I was not aware of it at all.

Coroner - As regards the terms upon which he and his wife lived, were they ordinary domestic terms?

They were very affectionate. From time to time, she was moody and, if I may say so, somewhat difficult.

Coroner - Do you know that she had taken an interest in her husband's business?

She had his interests very deeply at heart.

Coroner - It follows therefore that she would share his disappointment at his not being on the board ?

Yes, she felt it very acutely.

Coroner - Do you know from what you heard from him what his attitude was about his wife interfering in his business affairs?

It very greatly distressed him. He had loyally accepted the decision of his colleagues, but she would not accept it and caused him considerable difficulties, which greatly distressed him.

Coroner - Suppose your brother had discovered that his wife had been round to various newspaper offices endeavouring to interest them in his not being on the board, can you tell me what the affect would probably have been upon him?

I believe that if that had come to his knowledge he would have been exasperated beyond measure. I believe, I would go as far as to say, it would have turned his brain.

Coroner - Do you know of any other trouble which might have supplied an adequate motive for his taking his life?

I know of nothing else.

Coroner - Would the loss of the directorship be more serious to him from the point of view of finance or pride?

It was pride only, not finance.

The next witness was the nursemaid, Ruth Buckle who was in no doubt that the Brunners were quite happy and in a relaxed mood when she last saw them in the nursery a few hours before their deaths. She said that she did not hear revolver shots despite the nursery being above and only one room removed from the bedroom in which the bodies were discovered.

'Between' maid, Bella Scott, 15, of Northwich, was the last person to see the Brunners alive and she too confirmed that they appeared to be on 'good terms' on the night of their deaths. She said that the Prince had left for a holiday on July 9th, and the Princess had followed on July 23rd. From that date Mrs Brunner had, more or less, been in charge of Green Cottage. Mr Brunner had stayed at the house during two weekends prior to the tragedy.

Bella Scott - I opened the door when they came. I made tea and took it up to the writing-room.

Coroner - What were they doing?

They were sitting in front of the fire talking. Mr Brunner asked me to phone over for the chauffeur. That was about 6.50. Mrs Brunner said she would have her supper after Mr Brunner went about 8 o'clock. I reported that in the kitchen.

Coroner - And the next thing?

The hall bell rang. I went to the hall and Mr Brunner was

there. He said he wanted the chauffeur. The chauffeur came round and I went to the writing room. When I got to the writing room they both answered the door, saying, 'Hello, who's there?' Mrs Brunner said, 'Don't come in'.

Coroner - Did you hear any altercation?

No.

Coroner - What did you do then?

I went downstairs and told the chauffeur that I had told Mr Brunner he was there.

Coroner - When did you go up again?

About 9 o'clock. I went up two or three times and knocked at the door, but got no answer and came away.

Coroner - Did you hear any sound of a revolver?

No, sir.

Mrs Nellie Attwell, housekeeper/cook and wife of the Green Cottage butler, concurred with Ruth Buckle and Bella Scott that Mr and Mrs Brunner appeared quite friendly towards each other. The witness said she went upstairs because the maid, Bella Scott, could not get an answer.

Coroner - You went up to the room somewhere about 10 o'clock?

Yes.

Coroner - Were you the first to go in?

Yes.

Coroner - The light was on?

Yes.

Coroner - You thought they might have fallen off to sleep?

Yes. I felt uneasy and went back to the writing-room to have another look.

Coroner - You opened the door?

Yes.

Coroner - When you entered the room you saw Mr and Mrs Brunner on the floor between the foot of the bed and the writing desk?

Yes.

Coroner - You then went downstairs and called the chauffeur?

Yes.

Coroner - When the chauffeur came out of the room he said, 'It's finished'?

Yes.

The chauffeur Thomas Holdstock stated that on the day of tragedy he picked up Mrs Brunner at about 3pm and drove her to the Bath Club. Afterwards they proceeded to the city and he waited for an hour outside the Financial News office in Queen Victoria Street. From there they went to pick up Mr Brunner and drove to Green Cottage.

Coroner - What time did you get back?

About 6 o'clock. I asked Mr Brunner if he was going back to town, He said he would require me at about 8 o'clock. I went to have tea but a telephone message came over to my wife saying that Mr Brunner was ready to go back then. That would be about 7 o'clock. I drove to the cottage and got a maid to announce I was there. She said I must wait. I continued to stay in the car. As a rule, you could hear Mrs Brunner talking, but I heard nothing and it was very unusual to wait for Mr Brunner. Mrs Attwell went up to the room but could get no answer. It was now nearly 10 o'clock. She said to me 'Shall I open the door?' and I said 'Yes'. Mrs Attwell then called me in an agitated voice. I went up and saw Mr and Mrs Brunner lying at the foot of the bed. I was just going to shake Mr Brunner and tell him it was 10 o'clock when I noticed blood on the floor. I did not touch anything.

PC Thomas Whitwell then described how he found the bodies lying on the floor at the foot of the bed. Mrs Brunner, he said, was lying on her stomach, her face turned towards the bed, and Mr Brunner was lying across the body of Mrs Brunner on his left side, with his right arm round her waist. In his right hand he was holding a revolver. He was lying face down on Mrs Brunner. Both Mr and Mrs Brunner were fully dressed, and Mrs Brunner was wearing a hat and coat. PC Whitwell added that Mrs Brunner had a bullet wound on the right side of the neck, below the ear, and Mr Brunner a wound in his right temple.

Coroner - Were there any signs of a struggle?

No sir.

Coroner - Were there any writings bearing on the death?

There were notes all over the room, but not bearing on the death.

Dr Alexander Stowell of Northwich stated that he had been medical adviser to the Brunners for over fourteen years. He said he had attended Mr Brunner for a very severe attack of shingles on the face and scalp in August or September of 1925. Following this attack, Mr Brunner had suffered from very severe pains which had to be relieved by morphine. He had seen Mr Brunner from time to time until his death and on the last occasion he looked ill and worried.

Dr Stowell - Mr Brunner told me that there were times when he could not remember things, names or faces, and sometimes had to be prompted. I last saw Mr Brunner on October 27th. He was looking very ill and worried and said he was suffering from pains in the head and could not sleep.

Dr Athelstane Nobbs, Divisional Police Surgeon, testifed that upon arriving at Green Cottage he was able to ascertain that death had only recently occurred. In the writing-room, he said, there were untidy papers everywhere, but there was no sign of a struggle. Dr Nobbs then presented his post mortem report and photographs were produced by the police to show the interior of Green Cottage and, specifically, the writing-room.

Det. Insp. William McBride, who was responsible for the photography, noted:

There is a hat on the floor... a stain on the floor, between the foot of the bed and sideboard.

Summing up, the coroner said it seemed plain that Brunner had shot his wife and then himself. Worried to death, distracted and unable to sleep, he had finally thought of the revolver. He said:

He was a very distinguished business man, and had for many years been associated with the firm of Brunner Mond and for a time was chairman of this very important company. During his tenure of the chairman's office there was some financial trouble, not as regarded the stability of the firm of course, but some question of contract, or some trouble which resulted in heavy loss. As chairman of the board of directors he would no doubt be held responsible for that loss, and it would appear that it was on account of that unfortunate business transaction that he was requested to vacate the position of chairman of Brunner Mond & Company.

As you can well understand when that took place he would be very distressed, worried and unhappy. We know from the evidence of his medical adviser that he was so worried that he could not sleep, and that he was highly nervous, that he suffered from a well known nervous affliction, and was mentally confused and by no means normal. On top of this distressing question of the loss of his position as chairman, which was a matter affecting not his pocket as his pride, came the next blow.

There is apparently some huge combine of important business interests being formed, including Brunner Mond & Company, and when these large firms amalgamate, positions have to be found on the board for all the directors of the various companies which are amalgamated. When the new board was tentatively formed, or the names put forward, it did not include the name of Mr Roscoe Brunner. That information came to his ears on October 25th.

There again you can well understand what a blow that would be to his pride, coupled with the distress he must have suffered from losing the chairmanship... He procured the revolver, brought it to London, surely not with any intention of killing his wife, but with the intention of killing himself, and at this time was apparently not aware of the fact that his wife was actively intervening in the matter of his not having been placed on the board of the huge new combine. Can we not properly infer that on the night of the tragedy, the conversation in the writing room at Green Cottage must have been about the worrying absence of Roscoe Brunner's name from the Board of Directors of the new company. In the course of this discussion, is it not extremely likely as almost to amount to a certainty, that she then divulged what she had been doing, as she thought, in her husband's best interests, in the matter of hawking this grievance about the various newspaper offices? If that were so, does not that explain the whole tragedy?

Cannot you see what happened – a man driven to despair and distraction by losing his position finding his wife interfering in this way? Cannot you understand how, to a man of his temperament and his position that might well have been the last straw which caused his mind to lose its balance entirely? If so, his original intention of killing himself, which may be inferred from the evidence, seems to have been suddenly transformed, in a moment of intense frenzy, exasperation, and irritation, into an insane impulse also to kill his wife. If that is your view you will have no alternative but to return a verdict of murder in the case of Mrs Brunner, and of suicide while of unsound mind in the case of Mr Brunner. He was a frenzied madman, and yielded to an insane impulse, killing not only himself, but his wife.

Without so much as retiring to consider their verdict, the jurymen, in those days knowing their status in the presence of their 'betters', found exactly according to Ingleby Oddie's instructions. The following day, amidst what the newspapers described as 'utmost secrecy', the bodies of Roscoe and Ethel Brunner were conveyed to the crematorium at St John's, Woking... and their final journey was almost as intriguing and bizarre as the closing chapter in their lives.

From Wandsworth Mortuary, two enclosed cars carried the coffins on a long detour through Kingston, Esher and down the Porstmouth Road, before turning back to Woking and the crematorium which was circled twice. Cremation then took place behind locked doors and one assumes this was all designed to thwart further press interest.

Be that as it may, the proceedings took place with unseemly haste and one consequence was the absence of Princess Shelagh, who, apparently, had not returned from the Continent in time to attend either the inquest or the funeral service. Cremation in itself was unusual in Brunner family circles and three months later, with just three family mourners present, Roscoe and Ethel's ashes were formally interred in Lyne churchyard, to rest near to the grave of Roscoe's father, Sir John Brunner.

CHAPTER NINE
SEARCH FOR THE TRUTH

The late celebrated journalist Cyril Connolly, the inspiration behind James Fox's highly acclaimed book, 'White Mischief' which investigated the Kenyan mystery surrounding the murder, in 1941, of Lord Erroll, once wrote in the Sunday Times:

'Does it appeal to our vanity, the notion that logic or intuition or knowledge of the human heart can jump to the conclusion which has escaped all the experts and baffled the police? Or is it fear that injustice has been done and the wrong person convicted? Or that a murderer may still be at large? I believe those old teamsters, vanity and curiosity, play the strongest game, and that we all feel we can complete these jigsaws with human pieces'.

As far as the majority of mysteries are concerned, Connolly was correct, of course. However, the Brunner case was different, because if we are to believe the official version of events , there was never a mystery to investigate in the first place and yet the assumption is as irresistible today, as it was in some quarters at the time, that all was not as it seemed ...far from it!

A thorough examination of the available records and contemporary newspaper accounts conclusively reveals that most everything about this tragedy was superficial and that the inquest, with scant impartiality from the coroner, merely endorsed the most rational and logical explanation garnered by the police. It was a satisfactory conclusion, almost comforting, but it was nothing more because, in their anxiety to draw a veil over the affair and show it to be a straightforward 'husband murders wife and then commits suicide' scenario, the police and the coroner failed to consider the wider picture, the behind-the-scenes manoeuvrings surrounding the formation of I.C.I.; machinations that were, at best, relegated to peripheral importance.

Only the newspapers, in the days preceding the inquest, attempted to discover what had really been going on, but despite their obvious intuitivism, they did not manage a hint of the real story behind the Brunner deaths. For their efforts, of course, they were severely admonished by the coroner for what he considered to be their misguided and inappropriate speculation. And yet, ironically, prior to the inquest, the newspapers had advanced, almost to the letter, the same rhetoric, the same interpretation of events and reached precisely the same conclusions as the coroner himself. Typical was the Weekly Dispatch which succinctly summed it all up:

> What is the secret at the back of the terrible tragedy that has cost the lives of Mr and Mrs Roscoe Brunner, the millionaire commercial magnate and his beautiful wife? One would have thought that these two victims of a mysterious fate had practically everything that life could offer. Mr Brunner was the son of the late Sir John Brunner who, with Dr Ludwig Mond, built up the world-famous concern of Brunner Mond and Co., who own the great chemical works at Northwich, in Cheshire.
>
> For nearly thirty years Mr Roscoe Brunner was practically the head of this concern. His tastes were simple. His home life was happy.
>
> He was married to a beautiful and vivacious Irishwoman, the daughter of the famous Irish K.C., the late Dr Houston, who, after building up a big practice in Dublin, came to the English Bar and gained a splendid reputation there. His intellectual qualities passed on to his children. Mrs Brunner was a brilliant woman. She interested herself in social welfare work. The world was at her feet. Who could suppose that so terrible an ending was in store for her?
>
> Everything looked as though the Brunners, released from the ties and burdens of business, were about to enter upon a new lease of life and enjoyment. No-one dreamed that the dark shadow of death was already looming over what should have been a great, a stately, and a happy home. But apparently the Brunners were not happy. For nearly thirty years they had lived in a provincial industrial town, the husband absorbed in his work and the wife devoting herself to helping him in it and looking after the social welfare of the workers.
>
> She was the Lady Bountiful of Northwich. Fitted in every

way for the pomp and glittering fashionable society, allied to a princely family, wealthy beyond the dreams of avarice, witty and brilliant, born to adorn whatever circles she moved in, she deliberately turned away from the lure of society and identified herself absolutely and wholeheartedly with her husband's interests.

Then the first hint appeared of the tragedy that was to darken her life. He husband's health began to give way. It got so bad that he had, greatly to his regret, and to hers, to resign his position as chairman, in which he was succeeded by Sir Alfred Mond, M.P.. Apparently he worried incessantly over this. He was obsessed by a feeling that he was no longer to be of use in the world; she that she would not be any longer the Lady Bountiful of Northwich. Then came the great merger of big chemical firms with a capital of nearly sixty million pounds. To his great regret Mr Roscoe Brunner, a commercial magnate of European reputation, found no seat reserved for him on the board. He felt it acutely. His wife felt it perhaps even more. Apparently she insisted on discussing the details of his business with him, 'talking shop', as the phrase goes.

She believed, apparently, in pushing her husband on in the world of business. Whether this was discreet in his state of health, practically on the verge of a nervous breakdown, is a matter of which opinions may differ. The night before the tragedy Mrs Brunner herself appears to have had a nerve-crisis. She rushed off to the City, calling on newspaper editors and urging them to do something about the omission of her husband's name from the directorate of the new combine. She seemed to think that it lay within the functions of the newspaper editors to organise directorates of companies - the conception, apparently, of a woman novelist! She seemed to think that the merger was unnecessary and above all that it would hamper the social work she and her husband had done among the firm's tens of thousands of workers. There are some men who resent intensely, and almost furiously, the effort of a wife to control or direct them, who decline, in Stephenson's phrase, to go through life like smiling images pushed from behind. Mrs Brunner, blinded by her love for her husband, quite failed to realise that intrusion and dominance in his business affairs might drive him quite off his mental balance.

The newspapers were of one voice and when compared, it is glaringly apparent that all the reports must have emanated from the same, identical source. It was as if, in modern parlance, a 'spin' had been cleverly placed on the affair, to ensure that everyone, not least the coroner, would heap the burden of guilt squarely on Ethel Brunner, i.e. that she was solely to blame for the tragedy because she had interfered in her husband's business affairs.

A highly effective strategy, it worked perfectly and once the formalities were complete, even the journalists, bound by an ever-shifting quest for sensationalism, quickly lost interest. The Brunner deaths were simply consigned to the archives.

*****

From the outset, attempts to piece together the Brunner case appeared to be intrinsically flawed for, unlike Cyril Connolly's research into the Lord Errol murder, there seemed neither official documentation on public deposit, nor surviving witnesses. Therefore, the starting point in attempting to acquire documentary evidence centred upon the coroner, Samuel Ingleby Oddie, who was unique in his day in that he simultaneously served as coroner for three separate London areas, including the South Western District which covered Roehampton.

Born in 1869, Ingleby Oddie studied medicine at Edinburgh University, coincidentally at exactly the same time as Sir Alfred Mond, and after a period in the Naval Medical Service, took up general practice in New Malden. He then read for the Bar and in 1901 was called by the Middle Temple, subsequently practising at the Central Criminal Court where, notably, he worked with the prosecution on the famous trial of Dr Crippen.

As Coroner for Westminster, he fostered a reputation for controversy and long before the high-profile Brunner case he had seen his fair share of national headlines, particularly when drawing prominence to London's drug trade at the end of the First World War and also when investigating the assassination of Field Marshall Sir Henry Wilson.

Prior to 1927, coroners were not legally obliged to retain inquest papers, but a very small number have survived because the details of

Ingleby Oddie

some cases were considered particularly interesting or unusual. It was a long shot, but just possible that Ingleby Oddie had preserved the Brunner file at his office in Westminster. Unfortunately, all lines of enquiry were quickly expended when the present-day Coroner's Office, at Battersea, confirmed, emphatically, that the Brunner papers no longer existed.

As to the official Metropolitan Police file, quite astonishingly, this was to remain out of reach, at the Public Record Office, in Kew, because of what was described as 'sensitivity' which, according to established criteria, generally applies to criminal papers containing personal information relating to surviving individuals, normally relatives. The police have always held the responsibility for recommending the extent of a closure period and staff at the Public Record Office did not have access to the papers. Furthermore, there was no appeals procedure, even though most other criminal files, post-dating the Brunner case, were already open.

There was one other exceedingly odd fact with regard to the Brunner file. In cases of violent crime, i.e. those outside of State security, carried a virtual automatic seventy-five-year restriction period, but someone in 1926 at the Metropolitan Police had clearly ordered that the Brunner file, relating to a supposedly straightforward domestic tragedy, should be classified under Britain's 'Hundred Years Rule', with Royal and Government Cabinet papers. It was closed until the year 2026.

To put this into context, most modern 'crime' files, unless the police consider there are extenuating circumstances, are open to the public after thirty years. So what was so special about the Brunner file and why was it to remain on the 'secret list' beyond the release, for instance, of Cabinet papers relating to such momentous national events as the Abdication of Edward VIII and the Second World War? It beggared belief.

To make matters worse, there was no way of establishing why this additional cloak of secrecy had come to be thrown around the Brunner case and we were left only to speculate that it was either innocent over-zealouness by a senior police officer, or it smacked of influence, vested interest, an extraordinary measure to hide much of what had gone on.

Fortunately, in modern times, the rules concerning police files have generally eased and, following some considerable pressure, it was discovered that under new initiatives towards more transparent government, the Metropolitan Police was reviewing some selected, long-standing closures. By a remarkable coincidence, one of these was the Brunner file and four months later it duly went on public desposit.

The inquest proceedings referred to in this book are taken principally from the police shorthand transcript contained in the file, extensively cross-checked against reports in the London Times and other national, regional and local newspapers which, in those days, were exceedingly more accurate and verbatim in their reporting, especially of high-profile proceedings.

Most everything exists that one would expect within the yellowing Brunner file, but it still leaves almost as many questions as it answers. Witness statements taken at Green Cottage on the night of the tragedy make up the bulk of the papers and there are newspaper cuttings, a report of the inquest and assorted correspondence, but there is neither photographic evidence, which was certainly referred to during the inquest, nor a post mortem report.

There is also a clear indication that some material is missing. On the flysheet of the file there is a most intriguing note, relating to correspondence written ten years after the tragedy. A letter had apparently been received from a 'Mr J.H. Patterson' and to which the Metropolitan Police formally responded on May 22nd, 1936. The file note states:

'It is rather ridiculous that the writer should bother the police with an enquiry such as this, but we have the information and it is common knowledge, and we might say that the late Mr Roscoe Brunner was found shot at Roehampton.'

There is no indication of who J.H.Patterson was, or the nature of his query, for neither the letter, nor the police reply, are contained in the file. What does appear is a curious letter to Brigadier General Sir

William Horwood, the Metropolitan Police Commissioner. It read as follows:

My dear Sir William

I should like to convey to you my sincere thanks for the great kindness which we have received from Superintendent Hawkins and Detective-Inspector Eve over the Inquest yesterday. Both Superintendent Hawkins and Detective-Inspector Eve were most helpful in every way, and as Chairman of Brunner Mond & Coy. Ltd., and of the Imperial Chemical Industries Limited, I would like to thank you and ask you to be kind enough to convey our thanks to them.

On the face of it, rather innocuous, but it was from Sir Alfred Mond who was either being overly courteous or downright Machiavellian. As we shall see, he had managed to distance himself from the official proceedings and yet his avuncular hand and influence was everywhere, even to the extent that in the official public records, the Brunner case came to be mistakenly catalogued under the heading, 'Murder of Ethel Mond and suicide of Roscoe Mond'.

At the time of the deaths, Mond had been visiting Cheshire and upon his return to London it is documented that he hurriedly met with Roscoe Brunner's brother, Jack, to discuss, amongst other things the business implications of the tragedy. The goings-on behind the I.C.I. merger were already being touted as a possible cause and Mond, no doubt anxious to dispel further speculation, certainly wanted attention deflected elsewhere. The upshot was that although the police had not even commenced to check out the theory, Jack Brunner emerged from their meeting to publicly declare that Ethel Brunner's visits to Fleet Street, as exclusively reported in the Daily Herald on that very morning, had so tormented his brother that he had been driven to commit murder.

To the journalists looking for a 'new line' it was a dramatic revelation and they were only too willing to hang on to his every word. More significantly, from the moment of Jack Brunner's statement, it is apparent that the I.C.I. merger, except for the tenuous link involving Roscoe and Ethel Brunner's wounded pride, paled into the background of the official investigation.

Meanwhile, Mond, at his own instigation, and as noted by several national newspapers, arranged to visit the coroner. The newspapers reported that as chairman of Brunner Mond & Company and the self-appointed public voice of Imperial Chemical Industries, he was sure to be an important witness at the inquest. They were wrong. He did not appear and one must conclude that either Ingleby Oddie decided that Mond's evidence would have had no impact upon the verdicts, or that as a former Government Minister, as well as a high-profile public figure, his presence in the witness box would have sparked a further round of media sensationalism and that was something they were both determined to avoid, at any cost.

Mond, of course, was not only shrewd, but a master of persuasion. His approach to the coroner in the first place was somewhat irregular and to have told, under oath, what he knew may have set the press hounds baying... and what then of his I.C.I. dream? He could have lied, and may have been prepared to do so, but, perhaps, by attacking Ingleby Oddie's Achilles heel, namely his antipathy of Fleet Street's attempts to conduct the inquest in the columns of the newspapers, he definitely invoked the infinitely more prudent alternative of publicly saying nothing. He certainly had much to stay silent about! Only the Daily Mail saw how the tide was running:

> Whether the whole story will be revealed at the inquest depends upon the course the coroner decides to adopt. He may not consider it necessary, or desirable, to go into matters which, it is understood, involve questions of high finance, the necessity for the rearrangement of the board of control of a great firm, and the payment of a sum stated to be more than £1 million.

CHAPTER TEN
A YOUNG MAID REMEMBERS

Quite by chance, in Brunner Mond's old home town of Northwich, a local newspaper published archive material concerning the deaths of Roscoe and Ethel Brunner. The article was no more than a brief summary of contemporary reports, along with a little contrived titillation and make-believe for the entertainment of readers and one or two older ones reminisced about the tragic turn of events in November 1926.

One young man who knew something of the circumstances of the case took particular notice and carefully cut out the article to send to his aunt, living in the neighbouring Cheshire town of Altrincham. In the same newspaper two weeks later, a letter appeared correcting some of the discrepancies in the Brunner report. It was signed by a 'Mrs Isabella Hockenhull' and it was clearly from someone who possessed an intimate knowledge of the events at Green Cottage, Roehampton, all those years earlier.

Could this possibly be the young maid Bella Scott, the last person to see the Brunners alive? It was certainly too good an opportunity to miss, but I cannot say who was more taken aback when I telephoned Mrs Hockenhull; she that someone was asking for Bella Scott, or me when she replied in the affirmative.

Only those who have spent years searching through dusty records, chased interminable, non-productive inquiries and ruminated for hour upon hour over this fact or that possibility, can appreciate the thrill of locating an eye-witness, more so as I had long believed that all the principals had probably long since died. When we first met in her retirement flat, Bella Scott had just celebrated her 82nd birthday, a lovely, kind-hearted lady, gifted with marvellous memory of those far-off days when she was barely out of school and went to work for the Brunners. Her innocence of youth often meant she was not privy to some of the household gossip engaged in by the more established, older servants and, as she frequently pointed out in our conversations - 'You knew your place!'

The following is a fascinating account of Bella Scott's recollections of the Brunners, Belmont Hall, Northwich, and Green Cottage, Roehampton. With the exception of a few minor points, the details which she recalled of the tragic evening of November 3rd, 1926, are amazingly accurate when matched against the formal statement which she made to the police less than two hours after the bodies were discovered.

We lived in Great Budworth and Belmont Hall was the centre of the village. Everyone worked there and most of those who didn't were employed at Brunner Mond & Company. The Brunners were the gentry and as a girl I used to see them passing by in their car, or their daughter Shelagh Brunner riding out on her horse. She was certainly no beauty - I suppose you might say, a bit nosy. After the 1914-18 war, the village peace celebrations were staged in the grounds of Belmont Hall and as I was a maid of honour, it was my duty to present Mrs Ethel Brunner with a bouquet, on the steps of the hall. I remember I wore a mob cap and she told me I had beautiful hair and that I should let it hang down. She was very charming, but I wasn't sure if she was poking fun at me. When I left school at fourteen, my father went to see Mrs Brunner and I was offered a position as a maid in London, at Green Cottage, with Shelagh Brunner and her husband, the Prince of Liechtenstein. It seemed a very long way and my mother said if I didn't like it I could come back home when I had saved up the one guinea train fare. I did save the fare, but I decided to keep the money. My wages were £12 a year and I was paid monthly. Green Cottage was what you might call these days, a suburban house. It wasn't very large and the servants often wondered why the Prince and Princess lived in somewhere quite so small for their standing. But it never bothered them; they were always away. There was a cook/housekeeper, a housemaid, a parlour maid and myself and when Shelagh's baby, Christopher, was born I became between-maid, helping with normal duties and assisting the nursemaid when required. It wasn't a large domestic staff compared with other households of that time. The Prince and Princess liked to live it up and when it was Royal Ascot, or Wimbledon, large hampers would arrive from Fortnum and Mason. They drove a Lagonda and mixed socially in the highest classes, but these were the halcyon days after the 1914-18 war. It was a different world then. The Prince wanted a gentleman's gentleman and Leonard Attwell was appointed; he was ex-Coldstream Guards. The first cook-cum-housekeeper retired and so his wife, Nellie, came with him to take on those duties.

Almost as soon as the baby was born, the Prince and Princess were off on their travels again and Mrs Brunner came to run Green Cottage, also to look after her and Mr Brunner's own move to Roehampton Court. We were very near to Richmond Park and the garden of Green Cottage ran down to Roehampton Court. It was a grand looking man-sion. The butler, Harold Dorrington and his wife came to live in at Roehampton Court, to organise the furnishings and effects as they arrived from Belmont Hall. Holdstock, the chauffeur, and his wife were also there. Holdstock and Dorrington were very friendly.

Green Cottage had a lovely dining room and a lounge open-ing out onto what we would now call a patio, with an orna-mental pool. The house and all the furnishings were rented. Mrs Brunner lived upstairs, almost using it as a bed-sitter. She was an authoress and she liked to give off a certain aura; she said she wanted peace and quiet for her writing. That was Mrs Brunner though. It was said that a lot of her friends used to snigger behind her back about her novels. Not to put too fine a point on it, she was a bit of a bitch and she dominated Mr Brunner who loved her dearly; he let her have all her own way and the money to do it, but then Mr Brunner was a real gentleman. She was always trying to impress and was not well liked.

Mr Brunner suffered with shingles and often forgot things. He had a habit of tapping his forehead and I've heard her say - 'Ros, when you've finished tapping your forehead, I'll get on with my dinner.' She was that type of woman.

On the night of the tragedy, I took up tea to the writing room and later there would have been eggs and mushrooms for Mrs Brunner. They both seemed fine and I returned downstairs; the kitchen, the butler's pantry and the scullery were all underneath the stairs, down a few steps from the ground floor. I was in the kitchen and heard the door bell go. I went to see who it was and Mr Brunner was there. He said he had been outside to look for the car and would I telephone Holdstock to say he wanted to leave right away.

Holdstock came and I went upstairs. They were a bit startled when I knocked, perhaps preoccupied, but they certainly both answered. Holdstock was waiting in the kitchen and couldn't understand why the 'boss', as he called him, had not come down; he was always so punctual. Eventually, Holdstock said he would go up himself. He knew them better and, after all, it was the bedroom and, he said, I was a bit young. The next thing, he came back downstairs and he told me to stay in the kitchen whilst he went to fetch the police. I didn't really know what was going on and I don't suppose I really appreciated the seriousness of the situation. Eventually, two detectives arrived and interviewed me in the dining room, right below where it had happened. I don't recall a great deal about what was said, but I hadn't heard any gunshots, or an argument. What does stick in my mind is that the police said Mrs Brunner had been wearing a wig and really didn't have much hair. Wigs were fashionable and she used to have them laid out like fans; 'transformations' they used to call them. Queen Mary made them famous. Mrs Brunner had wardrobes full of clothes and hundreds of pairs of shoes, I know I tried a few of them on; she was just my size. When they were closing down Green Cottage, Dorrington's wife gave me a couple of pairs of shoes, but when I took them home to Great Budworth my mother threw them on the fire; she said I wasn't walking round our village in those because everyone would know where they had come from. With all the publicity and the inquest reports, I was quite a local celebrity for a while.

Shelagh and the Prince never lived in Green Cottage afterwards. It was all so sad. Mr Brunner was such a fine man, maybe too much of a gentleman. He had attained status through merit and we all knew that Sir Alfred Mond for one was deeply jealous. I learned afterwards that Ethel Brunner considered Mond conniving and ruthless, but it was not a view shared by Mr Brunner. I think he was out of his depth with Mond. Mrs Brunner hated Mond's guts and there had been rivalry between them for a long time.

Mr Brunner occasionally came to Green Cottage and usually stayed a few hours, but would then return to his apartment at Cavendish Square. He didn't stay overnight very often. I remember on one occasion helping serve a meal and hearing him say - 'Ethel, amalgamation is the workingman's ruin and it will see Northwich in the gutter'. It was all so sad. Ethel Brunner was too easily made the villain of the piece.

Two days after the tragedy, Bella Scott received a telegram from the Coroner's office instructing her to attend the inquest at Wandsworth Baths. She had kept the telegram all those years, along with a Brunner Mond & Company Golden Jubilee Mug, with the portraits of Sir John Brunner, Dr. Ludwig Mond and Roscoe Brunner. For seven decades she may also, unwittingly, have held the key to unlock some of the mystery surrounding the Brunner deaths.

Sir Alfred Mond with Queen Mary and the Prince of Wales.

Brunner Mond's heavy chemical industry in Cheshire.

CHAPTER ELEVEN
AN 'INTERFERING' WOMAN

In the accusatorial system of justice which is practised in England, it is the prosecution which has to prove guilt, beyond a shadow of doubt, but inquest proceedings are different and, by their very nature, are not generally open to interpretation and a battle of wits between opposing counsel. It is essentially the coroner's duty, largely acting upon inquiries carried out by the police, to establish formal identification and, without prejudice, to ascertain the circumstances of how a deceased person came by his, or her, death.

Factors from years earlier can often have a significant bearing on an ultimate verdict, though, to be fair, the difficulty in 1926, contrasting markedly with modern procedures, was that the authorities were under considerable pressure to bring matters to a conclusion within a few days, particularly in cases of likely murder where the apparent assailant had also perished. That is not to say, of course, that in the Brunner case, the police would, in any event, have turned up significant new evidence. They were too sure of themselves and they were not prepared to look much beyond the final twenty-four hours in Roscoe and Ethel Brunner's lives.

Consequently, the evidence as presented to the inquest became grossly distorted and, at times, scarcely believable. It started from a presumption of guilt against Ethel Brunner and by the time it had finished, she was officially portrayed as an interfering, belligerent woman who had provoked her sick husband to the point of despair. The business difficulties and the disappointments were not properly considered and the suggestion, that Roscoe Brunner, in an instant, had degenerated into a cold-blooded killer, was totally at odds with witness accounts. In fact, the more one studies the case, the more it becomes apparent that the police logic was built on sand, a mere interpretation of the objective facts, whilst the coroner, probably feeling compelled to show that he understood clearly what had taken place, furnished the jury with a hopelessly inadequate explanation that at least appeared reasonable.

The police, an indignant coroner and, particularly, Jack Brunner and Sir Alfred Mond were all eager to close the file on a messy and extremely embarrassing affair and not a single doubt was ever raised, not a question asked that had not already been answered in the newspaper columns. Yet, as a careful analysis of the available evidence reveals, it was not enough for the police and the coroner to weight the balance of blame in Ethel Brunner's direction, solely on the basis that she had somehow signed her own death warrant by calling upon the newspapers to complain about her husband's omission from the board of Imperial Chemical Industries. It was all too convenient, all too neatly packaged, a simplistic version of events.

The principal officer that night was 44-year-old Detective Inspector Albert Eve who had served with the Metropolitan Police since 1902, rising to the rank of inspector in 1920. By trade a bookbinder, he was honest and diligent, but generally uninspiring as a detective and, rather than heading a murder inquiry, he was probably better suited to more routine matters of police work.

Unfortunately, Eve was in the driving seat at Green Cottage and within a few hours of his arrival, at about midnight, he established conclusions from which he, and therefore the coroner, never waivered. In a formal telegram report, dispatched as early as 5.43am on the Thursday morning, Eve informed his Assistant Chief Constable that the case was 'undoubtedly murder and suicide' and that, as far as Scotland Yard was concerned, was effectively the end of the matter.

There was no urgency to detail a more senior, experienced officer to lead the investigation and Eve was left to pursue mere cosmetic inquiries and, for the sake of respectability in the subsequent handling of the inquest proceedings, tie up the evidence, no matter how circumstantial. Of course, the danger of a reliance upon circumstantial evidence, indirect proof, is that if one vital link breaks in the chain of suspicion, then the whole case invariably collapses. In the Brunner case, that one vital link was Ethel's visits to the newspaper offices.

Det. Insp. Eve, having contacted his superiors, had been left only with the problem of establishing what had tipped Roscoe Brunner's mental balance and turned such a mild-mannered, stoic man into a cold-blooded killer. Encouraged by Jack Brunner, he found what he believed to be the answer, in the Daily Herald's report of the interview that had taken place between the Night Editor and Ethel Brunner, approximately twenty-four hours prior to the tragedy.

This following is the Night Editor's own account. It was published in the newspaper on Friday November 5th:

It was one of those hours when visitors are least welcome in newspaper offices. A new edition was well under way. We were all straining in the recurrent race against time. When I was able to spare the few moments asked, I found awaiting me a middle-aged woman, plainly and inexpensively dressed in brown. She was handsome, blonde, blue-eyed, vivacious. Her speech was cultured, and she had a most attractive Irish brogue. Mrs Roscoe Brunner spread on the desk a copy of a financial daily newspaper. She pointed to a story giving particulars of the proposed merging of Brunner Mond & Co., the United Alkali Co., Nobel Industries and the British Dyestuffs Corporation.

'Have you noticed anything odd about that?' she queried sharply, almost challengingly. There was in her demeanour no excitement, no hysteria, no hint of impending tragedy. I replied that I had read all the news of the merger.

'Don't you see that my husband's name isn't there!' she exclaimed, placing her index finger on the list of directors.

'He has built up the Brunner Mond business. Old Sir John went into politics and left it to him. His life's work is in it... He has toiled there for $28\frac{1}{2}$ years...'

By 'Old Sir John' she meant the late Sir J.T.Brunner, Bart.

Drumming her foot rhythmically on the floor, Mrs Brunner went on to speak of her husband's scientific knowledge, of her share in his work, of her electing to live in a dreary industrial town when she might have moved in society, and luxuriated on the Riviera.

'We loved our workers!' she declared.

'I'm not concerned only for my husband. I tell you quite frankly I'm not a Socialist. But I feel very deeply about our workers at Northwich. We've done our best to look after them. We've maintained personal touch with them. Under the merger they are certain to suffer. Combines are soul-less.'

Then she digressed. With a flash of intellectual pride she spoke of her books, adding that she assumed that I had read 'Celia's Fantastic Voyage'. She told me that she was very busy on her new work. 'You must not think that I am a mere literary dilettante,' she continued. 'No-one is more interested in human causes than I am.'

Then from her reticule she drew a pink telegram form.

'Do you see this?' asked Mrs Brunner. 'It's about Spahlinger. That man has found the cure for consumption. I've done all I could to help him.

'What a tragedy!' she exclaimed, her eyes brimming with tears.

'Millions of sufferers, and that great and good man ready with his remedy, but unable to do his work because he has no money.'

Much else she said about her life and, affectionately, about her husband and her family. Now and again she would apologise for occupying my time.

'But what I have to say is so tremendously important! My husband doesn't know I'm here. He is at home, dining on eggs and bacon. He is a man of simple tastes.'

Reverting to the chemical industry, she spoke of the nitrogen fixation factory at Billingham-on-Tees, and of her part in acquiring it cheaply from the Coalition Government.

'There is nothing wrong with the industry,' she declared emphatically. 'It can more than hold its own. The merger is quite unnecessary.'

As we made our way down the stairs to the exit she continued to talk, briskly and vivaciously, about the merger and her husband. Outside was a large motor-car.

'Is that your car?', I asked.

'Yes,' was the reply. 'But I don't know how long it will be ours'.

Then she drove off into the fog and the night. What struck me most was that Mrs Roscoe Brunner was labouring under a strong sense of grievance. She was not wildly angry. She was not distraught. She had made up her mind to pursue a certain line at whatever cost to herself. Wifely love and solicitude were obvious in every word of what she said about her husband.

Later, when the police discovered that Ethel Brunner had also visited other newspapers offices, it seemed to perfectly fit the tragedy, especially as her conversation with the Night Editor of the Daily Herald was also, generally, the gist of what she had imbibed to the Financial News and the Daily Telegraph. She had been at the Herald at around eight o'clock on the Tuesday evening, the Telegraph office shortly before eleven, and at the Financial News on the Wednesday afternoon. Oddly, there is no record in the official police file of a statement from the Night Editor of the Daily Herald and we must assume that he was never actually interviewed by the police. However, there is a statement from William Underhill, of the Financial News, who recalled that Mrs Brunner had wanted the newspaper to publish her opinion of the merger, particularly her surprise and regret that her husband had not been invited to join the board. Underhill told the police:

On Wednesday November 3rd, 1926, in the afternoon, the Editor was engaged on very private business, which resulted in my attending to some callers. At about 4.30pm one of the messengers brought me in a note addressed in pencil to the Editor, and signed Mrs Roscoe Brunner. She was shown into the office and I greeted her as Mrs Roscoe Brunner. She stated that she would like the help of the journal in order to express her views of the big Chemical Combine (Imperial Chemical Industries Ltd). She deplored the fact that Brunner Mond and Company would lose its individuality by joining the Combine. She stated that for twenty six years Mr Roscoe Brunner, her husband, had worked very hard in the interests of the company and had done much to build up the company to its present strength. Further, that her husband was the prime mover in projecting the big Synthetic Ammonia Works at Billingham.

She herself had worked hard together with her husband taking a keen interest in the Brunner Mond enterprise at Northwich, Cheshire. She expressed her surprise and regret that her husband had not been invited to join the Board of the Imperial Chemical Industries, and she could not understand why. She pointed out that Sir Alfred Mond had really only been Chairman for a mere ten minutes - meaning only a short time - and that now he was handing over this great property to a combine. She said it would have been a great consolation to her and her husband had he been appointed to the Board of the new Company. She felt that he had been ignored, and she intended to get the matter raised in the House of Commons. She stated that as a shareholder, she would appeal to other shareholders to protest against the inclusion of the Brunner Mond interests in the Combine. When I first saw Mrs Roscoe Brunner, I formed the impression that she was somewhat agitated, but during the course of the conversation she grew calmer, and by the time she left my offices she appeared in better spirits... I have never seen Mrs Roscoe Brunner before. She seemed to be very level-headed and a sound businesswoman.

*****

It is said that unless a psychopath has been at work, there is always a motive for murder - greed, ambition, jealousy, lust, passion. Then, less easily defined, there is spontaneous anger, without premeditation... and it was, supposedly, his wife's visits to the newspapers that provoked spontaneous anger in the troubled mind of a depressed and confused Brunner. This, reasoned the police and the coroner, was the motive at the root of tragedy, as Ingleby Oddie put it to the inquest jury, the last straw which caused Brunner's mind to entirely lose its balance. But was he correct and does it square with the reality of events?

The answer is, most emphatically, 'no'.

Indeed, until Jack Brunner proffered the newspaper visits' theory, the police had been floundering on the question of motive. After all, there had been neither suicide note, nor witness to the deaths and, as far as Det. Insp. Eve was concerned, there was a distinct lack of clues to point him in the right direction.

The newspaper visits, surfacing as they did on the Friday morning, i.e. thirty-six hours after the bodies were discovered, therefore proved to be heaven-sent for the police who by then had less than three days to prepare a case for the inquest which was set for the following Monday.

In fact, apart from Ethel Brunner's marginally interesting choice of newspapers, Socialist, Conservative and Financial, her nebulous allegations, veiled references and innuendo concerning the situation into which her husband had plummeted, his resignation from the chairmanship of Brunner Mond & Company, the acquisition of the Synthetic Ammonia Works, at Billingham, and her reasons for continuing to live in a 'dreary industrial town', were not matters to concern the press. Nor, indeed were her perceived money worries which, in any case, were irrelevant. As their wills were later to reveal, Roscoe and Ethel Brunner together owned a considerable fortune, in cash assets alone of over £200,000, the equivalent today of several million pounds.

What remains an inescapable and fundamental truth is that the newspapers would have forgotten Ethel Brunner's visits, had she not have died in such violent circumstances. In fact, she had told them very little and to the courteously dismissive newsmen, she was perceived as nothing more than an embittered wife, caught up in her husband's business affairs. Yet, reinforcing the belief that the inquest was heavily staged-managed, none of the journalists were called to testify as to the lack of newsworthiness in what she had related to them and, consequently, the jury, and everyone else for that matter, was left to concur with the flawed conclusion that there had been considerable justification for Roscoe Brunner's spontaneous anger.

Viewed in isolation this may seem unimportant. After all, a visit to the newspapers was a visit to the newspapers, an attempt to hang out dirty linen in public and Roscoe Brunner may have felt enraged. But what this line of reasoning ignores are the wider implications of Ethel Brunner's behaviour. She was not fazed by the press, she was used to handling journalists, and, as her husband would have known better than anyone, she never did anything without a motive. So why had she told the newspapers so very little and are we to believe that this

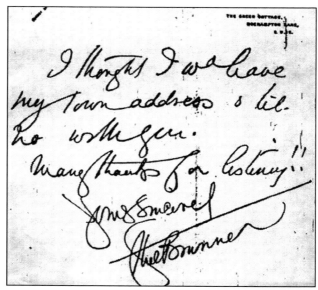

Ethel Brunner's note to the Night Editor
of the Daily Herald.

104

clever and calculating woman actually expected them to respond to her outpourings, such that they were? Of course not !

As will be revealed, the newspaper visits in themselves did not cause the tragedy, but they did ignite the spark. What the police and the coroner failed to recognise was that Ethel Brunner had other issues, more sensational, more newsworthy, to impart and that she had every intention of contacting the newspapers again.

As the Night Editor of the Daily Herald recalled:
> I was on my way back to my desk (after the interview) when another note was thrust into my hand. It was from Ethel Brunner and it simply stated - I thought I would leave my town address and telephone number with you. Many thanks for listening !!!.

Like William Underhill, at the Financial News, to whom she had promised to write a letter to the Editor, she was not done with the newspapers and a tragedy was in the making. The next time the journalists heard Ethel Brunner's name she was dead and the most enlightening insight into what may have been going on came, not from the police, but from an anonymous friend who told the press prior to the inquest:

> From what Mrs Brunner told me the last time I saw her, I think I can piece together the circumstances of their mental attitude which culminated in the tragedy. The origin of the trouble, as Mrs Brunner explained it to me, may be traced to a business deal that Brunner Mond & Co. had with another great firm. Mr Roscoe Brunner was chairman of his company at the time and, his wife told me, took the whole onus of the transaction on his shoulders. Later he resigned the chairmanship in favour of Sir Alfred Mond M.P.. This occurred during the General Strike and attracted little attention. The severance came as a great blow. Mr Brunner was tremendously proud of his firm, not only because he was the con-

trolling head of this enormous undertaking, but also because it gave him an opportunity of working intimately for the welfare of the thousands of their employees, by whom he was looked upon as a father. He was also very proud of the organisation of the undertaking, of the research work of the dozens of chemists they employed and of the firm's world-wide ramifications and high standing. Mrs Brunner was continually urging her husband to fight for recognition as one who had worked so hard at the head of Brunner Mond & Co., and went so far as to press him to challenge his company's actions in joining the combine. 'No-one will ever know,' she often emphasised to me, 'how I, a mere woman, helped him in his great efforts'.

CHAPTER TWELVE
STARTLING CAMEOS

The principal witness at the Wandsworth inquest was Roscoe's brother, Jack Brunner, who, in the footsteps of their father was a staunch Liberal MP and also a politcal ally of Sir Alfred Mond. Moreover, in order to smooth the way towards merger and ensure a degree of continuity with the old business, Mond had appointed him a director on the inaugural board of I.C.I.. He, therefore, had a vested interest where the deaths of his brother and sister-in-law might be perceived to impinge upon the sensitive negotiations which were taking place, precisely at this time, with the shareholders of the four companies who were about to be balloted on the I.C.I. merger proposals.

Like the coroner, who clearly inveigled the jury in order to spike the media's voluminous speculation and show that inquests are not conducted in the columns of the newspapers, Jack Brunner, whilst understandably wishing to protect the family name, seems to have been equally determined to suppress any connection between the affair and the merger. A straightforward domestic tragedy, the least said, the soonest mended, was as far as either of them was prepared to go. After all, someone had to take the blame and though they were satisfied that Roscoe Brunner had committed murder, it was his wife who was quite unjustly condemned.

Jack Brunner painted the blackest picture and, placing an implicit reliance on what he had to say, the coroner permitted, without challenge, every ridiculous and wildly inaccurate charge. It was a character assassination that turned the evidence on its head, to such an extent that the jury was bound to be prejudiced against Ethel Brunner.

How, for instance, could Jack Brunner have reached the conclusion that his brother had 'loyally accepted' his omission from the I.C.I. board of directors? Or, that Ethel, 'habitually meddling in business affairs', had turned her husband's brain by visiting the newspapers?

This was claptrap. Jack Brunner was not a medical expert to opinionate on matters of mental health and, furthermore, it was well known that he and his brother had not enjoyed a particularly close relationship in latter years, emanating no doubt from Jack's intense dislike of his sister-in-law. Indeed, by his own admission, and this was a crucial point in a case already reeking of complicity, he had not communicated with his brother following the Brunner Mond board meeting of Monday October 25th at which the I.C.I. directorship nominations had been approved. In short, he could not possibly have been aware of Roscoe and Ethel's reaction as events unfolded prior to that fateful evening of Wednesday November 3rd.

And as to Ethel Brunner's interference in business affairs, this was equally absurd. The inference was that she did so without the blessing of her husband and that it greatly antagonised him, but as we have seen, from as far back as the triumverate days at Belmont Hall, Roscoe Brunner never discouraged her involvement in business matters and even to the press, she was suggesting that she had played a significant role in helping Brunner Mond's strategic acquisition of the synthetic ammonia works at Billingham-on-Tees.

Just as important as what Jack Brunner said, was what he did not say, or at the very least, what he was not asked. Was Roscoe Brunner's omission from the I.C.I. board a consequence of his perceived poor health, or was it more to do with the business troubles concerning his humiliating resignation from the chairmanship of Brunner Mond?

Jack Brunner should also have been able to shed light upon the circumstances involving the I.C.I. board appointments and whether the situation had materially changed in the days leading up to November 3rd, or why his brother, so late in his career and despite his well known ambivalence towards London, had suddenly uprooted from his beloved Cheshire to start a new life in the capital?

These were pivotal questions, but such was the economy of truth at what may only be described as a sham of an inquest that the police had neither grasped nor considered them. Jack Brunner certainly did not want them raised and the coroner was adamant that the answers should never be made public.

Many friends and acquaintances of Ethel Brunner viewed with considerable unease that she was solely to blame for the tragedy and amongst numerous statements in the official police file there is one which forcibly makes the point. Significantly, it was procured not as a result of police investigations, but submitted voluntarily by a London psychiatrist, Haydn Brown, who stated:

> The illness of Mr Roscoe Brunner has been repeatedly referred to in the public press; but not the illness of Mrs Roscoe Brunner. She has many friends and relatives who might wish that the latter point should be taken into account, for various reasons. I first made the acquaintance of both ten years ago when Mrs Brunner was suffering from a kind of nervous disorder which is always extremely difficult to deal with. I was asked to undertake the treatment of her case by a leading London neurologist. Mr Brunner was then in a good state of health. After some months Mrs Brunner recovered, and she continued to be well until her husband's business affairs began to cause worry. Anxieties multiplied; meanwhile she could never be persuaded that her nervous system had again been affected. Anxiety neurosis and intense urge were the main features. A few weeks ago she wrote saying that she would come to London again, to see me with a view to treatment, recalling her former recovery. She did not come. She evidently felt that the further worries about business and the new house had better be fought through before she came to see me. Of late Mr Brunner had no power to persuade her on any point whatsoever; his expostulations only aroused her determination to be energetic all the more. I do not consider that Mrs Brunner had a bad temper, as reported. She was captivatingly and cleverly firm, also intensely energetic. Her later relationship with her husband just prior to the tragedy was quite an amicate, as seen in a great proportion of married people. It was more amicable than when I studied it ten years ago. She had

a high opinion of him; and he of her. The two had arranged to go abroad together on a happy mission before the tragedy.

Interestingly, Haydn Brown's statement was dated Sunday November 7th, plainly suggesting that he was trying to balance the furore which, by the weekend, had built up into a public crescendo against Ethel Brunner. He did not say it in so many words, but the inference is clear that he thought her role in the tragedy was being grossly overstated.

The coroner was not impressed. He was in no mood to tolerate a case for the 'defence', or to seek anything which might absolve Ethel Brunner, and so like Sir Alfred Mond, Haydn Brown, who had been acquainted with the Brunners for at least ten years and who could have spoken with authority about their relationship and also Jack Brunner's preposterous claims about the state of Roscoe's ill-health, was not called as a witness.

******

During the weekend following the revelations concerning the newspaper visits, the police had said: 'There is no doubt, or very little doubt, that Mrs Brunner's endeavours to enlist the newspapers for the purpose of airing her grievances, in all probability, incensed Mr Brunner beyond further endurance.'

Deplorably, the police did not seek to eliminate the 'very little doubt' they knew existed and, instead of remaining open to all avenues of investigation, it is patently obvious that in their eagerness to accept witness statements at face-value, a series of critical facts became hopelessly distorted and, in some instances, misinterpreted altogether.

The belief that they dismissed anything which did not accord with their own, and Jack Brunner's, version of events is reinforced by several startling cameos from Dr Athlestane Nobbs, the police surgeon.

When Nobbs reached Green Cottage, he found the body of Ethel Brunner lying face-down, more or less on her stomach, with Roscoe Brunner on his left side, his right arm encircling her waist and his right hand, still clutching the revolver, slightly, trapped beneath her hip. It was curious but the police, attributing the rather precise position of Brunner's hand to 'post mortem movement', preferred to share the view of those romantically inclined servants who thought the final position of the bodies showed that the Brunners were 'together in love to the end, inseparable'.

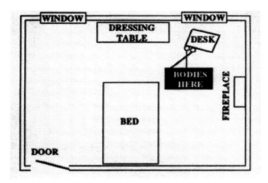

The investigating officers were convinced that Brunner must have instantly shot himself after killing his wife; that he had done so from a kneeling position and that the revolver was so small it had remained in his hand at the moment of death. However, this seems to be flawed logic for even if the shots were no more threatening than a book falling from a table, the balance of probability suggests there would have been some retort and the weapon would have slipped from his grasp.

Dr Nobbs had another, even more dramatic observation regarding the position of the bodies. He said: 'The thing that struck me most was that the drawer, against and under which their heads were, was open. It must have been opened by someone. I asked if anyone had opened the drawer, no-one had. It seemed curious to me that this should be. With the drawer open some nine inches above, it would have been virtually impossible for the bodies to have finished in the position in which they did.'

The coroner did not bother to probe the point. The open drawer, which, apparently, could be seen on police photographs of the death room, was inconvenient evidence and so it was set aside passed, unbelievably, without question. Yet it may have been crucial evidence. If the Brunners did not, or could not have opened the drawer, then who was responsible and did it occur before, or after, the bodies were discovered by the housekeeper? If the drawer was already open when Mrs Attwell entered the room, then there are more sinister possibilities to consider. On the other hand, if the drawer came to be opened after Mrs Attwell entered the room, then someone in the household that night was telling lies.

We know of the presence of five members of staff at Green Cottage - the maid, Bella Scott, the nursemaid, Ruth Buckle, the housekeeper, Nellie Attwell, the chauffeur, Thomas Holdstock, and the butler-valet Harold Dorrington.

Bella Scott did not move from the kitchen area after the bodies were discovered, whilst the nursemaid was asleep in her room, so much so that she did not find out about the tragedy until the following morning. The other three all entered the writing-room, but as to the housekeeper, it seems ridiculous to believe that in her state of shock upon discovering the bodies, that she would have stopped to open a drawer in the bureau. In fact, in her panic, she had actually fled from the house to find a policeman which she succeeded in doing, approximately half a mile away. P.C.Whitwell was on point duty in Medfield Street, Roehampton and, running towards him, Mrs Attwell shouted... 'Come at once to Green Cottage, something has happened.'

The constable and Mrs Attwell were then making their way back along Roehampton Lane when Holdstock pulled up in the Daimler, so begging an explanation as to what he and Dorrington had been up to in the intervening ten minutes, or why, curiously, the police had not been contacted directly from the Green Cottage telephone, whereas Jack Brunner most certainly had. From his home in Harrington Gardens, SW7, Brunner managed to arrive within minutes of P.C.Whitwell and almost an hour before the first of the detectives.

Holdstock and Dorrington were not questioned by the police on the 'missing ten minutes' and there is a strong suspicion that in their individual statements they were saying much less than they actually knew. Dorrington claimed that when the chauffeur received instructions, much earlier than expected, to take 'the boss' back into the city, he decided to accompany them 'for the ride' and later, he claimed, he and Holdstock had entered the writing-room together when Mrs Attwell had called out. Yet neither Holdstock, nor Mrs Attwell, mentioned Dorrington being there at all.

Holdstock said: 'I waited for about three hours, and eventually Mrs Attwell went into the writing-room, and when she came out she called for me to go up. I went up, entered the writing room, and there saw Mr and Mrs Brunner lying on the floor at the foot of the bed. Mrs Brunner was lying on her left side, and Mr Brunner was lying next to her with his arm across her body. They were both dead. When I saw Mrs Attwell I said, 'It's finished'. Mrs Attwell then went for the police. I was in and about the house from 7 o'clock ..."

One has to say, it was a rather odd reaction from Holdstock and the question is, do the words, "It's finished!", imply that to him the tragedy was not entirely unexpected? He was certainly neither shocked nor surprised.

A further puzzle was Ethel Brunner's reported black eyes which the inquest jury was left to infer had occurred because she was struck by her husband during a violent argument in the moments leading to the actual killing. On the other hand, the servants had not even detected raised voices whereas, in the past, they had often heard Ethel Brunner berating her husband, especially in the latter days at Belmont Hall when matrimonial arguments were hardly concealed from the domestic staff. Dorrington testified that the Brunners frequently argued, and over the most trivial matters. He said that Mrs Brunner occasionally confided in him and she was considerably worried over her husband being forced to give up the chairmanship of Brunner Mond & Company.

'She thought that the other partner (Sir Alfred Mond) was not treating Mr Brunner fairly,' he said.

Holdstock went even further to claim that Ethel Brunner was a woman of volatile temper who often resorted to 'violent language' against her husband. He also said it was not unusual, when waiting with the Daimler outside the front door of Green Cottage, to hear her

113

talking in the first-floor sitting room.

Yet on the night of November 3rd, and despite the fact that he had waited for the best part of three hours, he had not heard a single word uttered, let alone a quarrel during which Ethel Brunner might have been expected to have fired off a potent volley of abuse as her husband supposedly degenerated into a frenzied rage.

Considerably more disconcerting was the untidiness of the writing-room. P.C.Whitwell and Dr Nobbs both noted the disarray and said that correspondence and documents were strewn about the floor and furniture. Deplorably, the police, reasoning that the Brunners themselves must have been responsible, were not in the least bit interested and took the point no further. Yet, as the servants would have said, Ethel Brunner was unbearingly fastidious about the neatness of her living quarters and meticulous about her personal papers, and nor was she a woman to sit meekly by whilst anyone else, her husband included, rifled through her belongings. We are therefore left to conclude that the search of the writing-room could only have taken place *after* Ethel Brunner's death. There can be no other logical explanation and of all the mistakes made by the police, from false, hasty or insufficient observation, this was probably their most crucial. In due course it was to come back and haunt them.

Many details, as accepted by the police and the coroner, are profoundly hard to swallow, but the most intractable conundrum centred upon Roscoe Brunner's revolver which the coroner insisted had been acquired for the sole purpose of committing suicide.

'He had brought the revolver to London surely not with the intention of killing his wife, but with the intention of killing himself,' said the coroner.

Licensed with a firearms certificate in Northwich and a permit to hold two-hundred rounds of ammunition, Roscoe Brunner was the registered owner of the revolver, a tiny nickel-plated, five-chambered .32 calibre Smith & Wesson which was almost certainly a safety-first hammerless model, designed to be quickly removed from a pocket and fired at close range for self-protection.

Brunner had always kept the weapon in a small white medicine cabinet at Belmont Hall, in Cheshire, but over many years it had fallen into disrepair. In July, 1926, exactly at the time of the domestic upheaval associated with his permanent move to London, he person-ally called at the Bond Street (London) gunsmiths, Holland and Holland Ltd. and, as instructed, the revolver was cleaned, put into action and returned to Belmont Hall on July 23rd. According to Harold Dorrington, it was put back into the white medicine cabinet. Later, the police discovered that Brunner had transferred the weapon to his apartment at Cavendish Square where, in a locked drawer, they found thirteen cartridges and some cleaning equipment.

There is a glaring contradiction here. If Roscoe Brunner, as suggested by the coroner, was not aware of his wife's newspaper vis-its, and upon impulse became an insane killer, why did he carry the revolver, fully loaded with five bullets, first to the Bath Club and then to Green Cottage?

These were muddy waters, but neither the police nor the coroner were anxious to delve too deeply to seek the truth which was further confused by Det Insp Eve reporting to his superiors, erroneously and without corroboration from a single witness, that prior to killing his wife, Brunner had deliberately gone downstairs to retrieve the weapon from the pocket of his overcoat.

It simply did not make sense and amongst many discrepancies, the revolver presents some of the most nagging questions of all. The only sure fact that we can deduce is that when Brunner had taken the weapon to be put back into working order, in the July, the I.C.I. merger proposals were not even a whiff in the London air and nor is there any reason to suppose, at that time, he was planning to take his own life. He could only have had self-protection on his mind.

Later, of course, the situation may have changed, but it was ludi-crous of the coroner to suggest that on the night of the tragedy, and because of his omission from the I.C.I. board, eight days earlier, Brunner had the revolver in his pocket expressly to take his own life... i.e. not in the privacy of his Cavendish Square apartment, but ostensi-bly in full view of his wife and the servants at Green Cottage!

This was absurd and what the inquest should have considered was did Brunner set out that night to murder his wife, or was he, for whatever reason, paranoid for his own safety?

One who might have assisted with the police inquiries was Alfred James Robinson, the butler-valet at Belmont Hall. During the period when his colleague Harold Dorrington was assisting with the Brunners' move at the London end, Robinson had remained to oversee the closing down of Belmont Hall. According to his daughter, Mrs Ivy Pickup, of Northwich, her father received a telephone call from Roscoe Brunner, instructing him to procure the revolver from the white medicine cabinet and send it with all haste on the very next train to London. Robinson did exactly as he was bid and personally delivered the package, containing the weapon and ancillary equipment, to the local mainline station near Northwich. It was addressed to Brunner at Cavendish Square and though Mrs Pickup cannot be exact, she is certain that her father told her that he received the telephone call 'not much more than a day before the tragedy'.

The police failed to interview Robinson, but if his account of the timing is correct, and there is no reason to suppose otherwise, then it tallies uncannily with those cataclysmic final twenty-four hours in which Brunner, out of desperation, was provoked into sending for his revolver.

CHAPTER THIRTEEN
GAME OF BRINKMANSHIP

To winnow some of the facts from the falsehoods, to discover how it all went wrong for the Lady Bountiful of Belmont Hall, we must consider national events from December 1923 and the historic General Election that saw Britain's first Labour Government rise to power. Sir Alfred Mond, the former Minister of Health in Lloyd George's Coalition, was out of office, rejected by the voters of Swansea, and within a matter of days of his election defeat he was reappointed onto the board of Brunner Mond & Company. His return to industry had never really been in doubt, only the timing and, anyway, his closest associates generally agreed that his talents were best suited to the boardroom, always provided, of course, that his fellow directors were prepared to be ruled by an autocrat and that he could bring all his authoritarian powers to bear, free of the restrictions and untramelled by any need to seek the approval of the electorate.

The thought of a downtable directorship was no more appealing to Sir Alfred Mond than was a place on the backbenches in the House of Commons and, in any case, as he saw it, Brunner Mond was managed by what he termed a 'preponderence of exceedingly puzzle-headed men' and he was contemptuous of many of the directors and their policies.

Recognised as one of the most incisive minds brought to bear on British industry of the 1920s, Mond surveyed the scene of Britain's industrial landscape and saw the nation's basic industries - shipbuilding, coal, cotton, heavy engineering, iron and steel - in the grip of depression. Amongst the few who were riding the storm was the chemical industry, but he was convinced that with himself at the head and through radical reorganisation he could place it on a truly international scale.

First he had to manoeuvre himself into a position from where he could not only influence, but control the future direction of the industry and Brunner Mond offered him that opportunity for at the very moment of his return, the company was about to become embroiled in the final, disastrous legal battle with Lever Brothers in what came to be the catalyst for the tragedy at Green Cottage two years later.

The game of brinkmanship between Brunner Mond and Lever Brothers had been a thorn in the side of both these industrial giants for over ten years and, in March, 1924, it finally plummeted into open warfare when William Hesketh Lever personally asked Roscoe Brunner if it was true that Brunner Mond had been reneging on agreements over the sale of alkali to other soap manufacturers. Initially Brunner indignantly denied the allegation, although, privately, Hesketh Lever was adamant that he had received 'reliable information' confirming that he was being sold short.

In a letter to one of his colleagues, he wrote: 'Without mentioning names, except that I do not include the present or past Chairman of the Company in this remark, there is an entirely changed atmosphere towards the contract... I feel very uneasy and uncomfortable because I am satisfied we are not today getting a square deal as we were entitled to under the contract.'

It seems that Hesketh Lever was pointing the finger at Roscoe Brunner's triumverate lieutenants, J.G.Nicholson and J.H.Gold as being the unmentionables, but he would probably have never been able to prove the charge and there the matter may have rested. However, exactly one week later, Roscoe Brunner dispatched an amazingly frank letter, confessing that Brunner Mond had indeed not been charging one customer the full amount for their alkali, in flagrant breach of an agreement with Levers. Even more deplorably, Brunner Mond had been drawing up bogus invoices to deceive their own auditors whose certificates Levers had agreed to accept as evidence of prices charged.

It was an astounding, seemingly reckless revelation and, on the face of it, either an act of an absurdly naive chairman, an unlikely prognosis, or a calculated gamble to defuse what was potentially the most serious of all the disputes which Brunner Mond and Levers had fought. Legally trained that he was, Roscoe Brunner must have realised that his admission would lead straight to court, but what he could never have envisaged were the incredible personal repercussions.

The general opinion at the time on the Brunner Mond board, and since reiterated by the I.C.I. historian, W.J. Reader, was that in writing so quickly to Levers, Roscoe Brunner's nerve broke, an assumption which, in the absence of other mitigating evidence, appears to be a reasonable explanation for what was undoubtedly a gross act of folly. So were Roscoe Brunner's fellow directors correct, or did other powerful forces influence him? Indeed, did he jump or was he pushed?

What was widely accepted was that his initial letter of denial had not been approved by the board of Brunner Mond, but one wonders whether the response to Levers would have been any different if it had been? After all, the fraud had been going on for years and there must have been other directors who were at least as culpable as Roscoe Brunner. Certainly Hesketh Lever thought so, but ultimately only J.H.Gold and Brunner ever paid the penalty.

If he had known all along that Brunner Mond was reneging on the Levers' contract, and he was hardly unimpeachable in the matter, it goes almost without saying that Roscoe Brunner would have wanted to protect his own position in what was potentially the biggest crisis of his business career and, significantly, it was also the first time he had ever been called upon to tackle the old enemy without his father's guiding hand. Was he to ignore Levers' accusations, or was he to make a clean breast of it and hope that the consequences would not be too dire? This was Brunner's agonising predicament and, given his style of management, it is incomprehensible to imagine that he would have chosen to act independently.

So, to whom would he have turned for advice? Definitely not his trusted colleagues, Gold and Nicholson, who were also up to their necks in the same hot water, and not Jack Brunner who as a sitting MP had become rather remote from the business. The only possible boardroom associate would surely have been Sir Alfred Mond, the company's most powerful private shareholder, and what could have been more natural than for old friends and scions of the company founders to hold private discussions? Besides, no-one could ever have accused Mond of being anything less than liberal with his opinions.

Brunner probably felt confident that with Mond's support he could ride the storm and carry the board but, as events were to prove, he was embarking on a dangerous game. Mond's support amounted to little more than a wholesale betrayal, as, sub-consciously, half-consciously, Brunner fell into his clutches. His biggest mistake was in believing that Mond genuinely intended continuing his Parliamentary career, a notion which the former Minister had long since exhausted.

Levers felt they had little choice but to take the matter to law and, probably because of the acrimony of the past, the Brunner Mond board was quite prepared to make a fight of it. However, as the court action neared, it was Mond who took independent legal advice and it was he, through his cousin Emile Mond, who persuaded the Brunner Mond board to capitulate by accepting an out-of-court settlement, although, as we shall see, the litigious Mond, above all others, knew what the finest legal brains could achieve.

Initially, Brunner Mond offered £318,000, but it was rejected out of hand by Levers and in the end, a colossal sum of £1 million was agreed. Hesketh Lever did not live to witness his finest hour over his old adversaries but, ironically, the £1 million was exactly the amount which he had always considered he had been overcharged for the soap manufacturers, Crosfields and Gossages.

The most intriguing aspect of the final litigation proceedings with Levers, was the clandestine actions of the Brunner Mond board. A sub-committee of Sir Alfred Mond, Emile Mond and Jack Brunner, the latter a lone voice against settlement, was formed to deal with the matter and afterwards a confidential report on the affair was sealed in the presence of the full board and deposited in the company safe.

A copy of the report was also sent to Brunner Mond's solicitor, but both sets of documents carried the explicit instruction that they were never to be opened without a formal resolution from the board. What happened to this confidential report, and the nature of its contents, has never been revealed and even Reader, I.C.I.'s official historian, was perplexed as to why numerous archives relating to the Lever Brothers' settlement had simply vanished.

We will also never know who tipped off Hesketh Lever in the first place, although there is an overwhelming suspicion that Mond played a cunning role in precipitating events. The upshot was that Roscoe Brunner was unceremoniously dumped as chairman in favour of Mond, who then made a great public show of appearing to be grudgingly taking over the mantle of chairman. In truth, Mond had moved effortlessly into his new seat of power.

The secret details of the Lever Brothers' settlement, bringing the dispute to its costly conclusion, occured in January, 1926, at exactly the time that Mond was finally quitting the Liberal Party, effectively ending his career in mainstream politics. Two weeks later, Roscoe Brunner tendered his resignation and, given the sequence of events, is it so cynical to believe that he was cashiered from office, or that his fate was sealed from the moment that his reluctant successor made up his mind to return from politics to industry?

For Brunner, the retreat from the ignominy of the Lever Brothers' settlement was not as dire as may be supposed. It is true that in the late summer of 1925 he had been struck by the painful attack of shingles, to his face and scalp, a condition normally afflicting the over-fifties and activated by physical, or emotional stress, and for several months he was treated with morphine as the illness racked at his nervous system, bringing temporary lapses of memory and acute depression. Yet, as most anyone who has ever suffered from the complaint can testify, it is a condition which, without ever disappearing totally, does begin to diminish in its intensity.

This was certainly the case as far as concerned Roscoe Brunner for at the time of his resignation, and in spite of the intolerable business pressures he had been under for almost twelve months, he was feeling much better and one has to conclude that even though he may have taken the honourable course by falling on his sword over the Lever Brothers' debacle, his decision had little to do with acute ill-health. Indeed, he was absent from the board only for a few months leading up to Brunner Mond's 1926 annual meeting and afterwards actually chaired minor board meetings when Sir Alfred Mond was away on other company business. The mental scars and the heartfelt sense of injustice during his absence from direct business management came to be the most dismal period of Roscoe Brunner's life, but, even so, he could not be persuaded to consider the mildest retaliation against his detractors.

His wife on the other hand viewed matters differently. It was part of her nature and she had long regarded Sir Alfred Mond as a conniving opportunist who had unmercifully exploited her husband, the consequence of which was irrevocable damage to her own position in local society, for what was social standing without power, even for the mother of a European princess?

The Lady Bountfiul could no longer pick up the telephone and delight in answering - 'Mrs Roscoe Brunner, the wife of the chairman of Brunner Mond'.

So as the servants noticed, an intensely strained atmosphere began to pervade Belmont Hall as Ethel Brunner remorselessly pressed her husband to fight, to confront his accusers and, if necessary, to seek the support of the Brunner Mond shareholders. She was not averse to fighting dirty when needs arose and she was quite willing to start the mud-slinging, but for any attack to be successful, it required her husband to personally renounce Mond.

As ever, loyal and stoical, a good old-fashioned British stiff upper-lip gentleman, Brunner would agree to nothing more than private discussions with the new chairman.

Ethel Brunner deeply distrusted Mond's political games. He had always been a little too obsequious, too clever by half, and so it proved. Mond was a good listener, diplomatically unctuous, his astuteness honed over twenty years in Parliament where he had met and mastered greater adversaries than Roscoe Brunner and he simply glossed the way with sympathy and promises. This time not only Brunner fell under his spell, but Ethel as well... or at least as far as she was prepared to turn a blind-eye in order to realise her own cherished dreams and her desire to seek new horizons. Consequently, Roscoe Brunner did not attend the annual meeting and a confrontation was avoided as

Mond shrewdly paid tribute to his predecessor:

> Before passing on to the ordinary business of the company I
> feel it only right to explain my presence in the chair today. As
> you have already been informed in the report of the direc-
> tors, Mr Roscoe Brunner has, unfortunately, been feeling for
> some time the strain of the responsibilities of the position he
> has occupied for a considerable time, and I understand that
> he intends taking a well-earned vacation. You will, however,
> be pleased to know that he retains his seat on the board and
> his active interest in the affairs of the company and its sub-
> sidiaries. I am sure I am voicing the opinion of all in express-
> ing the hope that he will at an early date be restored to his
> usual health and activity. In consequence of this, my col-
> leagues requested me to take the position of chairman of the
> board. I felt I could not possibly refuse to accede to this
> request, although I fully realised the additional work it
> would impose upon me, but I can assure you that, having
> undertaken this very responsible task, I shall devote to it all
> the time and energy it requires.

What Mond did not reveal to the shareholders were his innermost
thoughts, bound as they were to a Brunner Mond alliance with the
Chemical & Dye Corporation, of America, and the Farben Group, of
Germany. Mond had always been one of the most likely public figures
to bring about conciliation and agreement between Britain and
Germany, but rather than building bridges he would have argued that
his manoeuvres were driven by pure business pragmatism.

The Farben Group was massive even by American standards. The
key was oil and in its simplest terms what Mond was planning was a
British holding company which would be able to determine control of
vast lucrative markets around the world. To entice the Germans to join
his international consortium, he was even prepared to cede to them a
major stake in Brunner Mond & Company, a move personally sanctioned by the British Prime Minister, Stanley Baldwin, under govern-

ment regulations still in force from the Great War. Mond had always thought it was his fate to be misunderstood, but with Baldwin's approval he was confident that he could handle his critics, as he had always done, either by staying aloof and ignoring them, or, if all else failed, by hauling them before the courts.

What he could not afford within the ranks of his shareholders was an insurrection against his chairmanship, marshalled by someone of the stature of Roscoe Brunner who remained a popular and respected figure.

The carrot which Mond must surely have dangled, and there can be no other explanation, was the promise of a senior directorship within the proposed holding company which he envisaged would be based in London and this, given his changing business fortunes and his steadfast opposition of the past, proved to be the over-riding consideration in persuading Roscoe Brunner to move to the capital. His previous reluctance was well known, as observed by a close business associate in the wake of the tragedy at Green Cottage.

'What I specially admired about Roscoe was the way in which he stuck to Northwich, although he had many temptations to lead a society life in London,' he said.

Brunner had been left with little choice in the matter. He could either drift into semi-retirement, or acquiesce to Mond's magic tongue, that weaver of so many forceful arguments across the floor of the House of Commons, and accept the opportunity to resurrect his business career away from his beloved Cheshire. He may have had grave reservations, but these were more than countered by his wife, who was so delighted at the prospect that she immediately set off in search of a fine house in which to lavishly entertain the indolent socialites of the metropolis. In the euphoria she had not forgotten the warning which she and Sir John Brunner had so often impressed upon her husband. Never trust Mond!

CHAPTER FOURTEEN

CHESHIRE TO LONDON

The Brunners' move to London coincided with the birth of their first grandchild, Christopher, to their daughter Shelagh and Prince Ferdinand who, following their marriage in 1925, had taken up residence at Green Cottage, in fashionable Roehampton, a middle-class bastion of suburban respectability. Functionally stylish and standing comfortably in its own grounds, tucked away behind high wooden fencing and rambling laurel bushes, Green Cottage had previously been occupied by a clergyman and his family and, by the standards of the day, was considered a modest dwelling. Not that it mattered to the Prince who, through his status and his connections, was a renowned womaniser and very much a figure of the Roaring Twenties' London scene, of wild parties and loose morals.

At the front of Green Cottage was Roehampton Lane and Queen Mary's Hospital, and, to the rear, the Mount Clare Estate and Richmond Park. Just off Roehampton Lane, and within a few hundred yards of Green Cottage, was Roehampton Court, a handsome Georgian mansion (now the Maryfield Convent). Built prior to the First World War, and similar in style to Belmont Hall, in Cheshire, it was described by the auctioneers of the day as having dignified proportions, tasteful fittings and a 'feeling of rest and harmony'. Fortuitously for Ethel Brunner, it came onto the market within weeks of her husband finally agreeing to transfer his business interests to the capital and she was immediately able to secure a lease on the property.

Soon, with her customary alacrity and penchant for pretentiousness, she began directing an extravagant programme of refurbishment and, as police inquiries were to reveal, Roscoe Brunner was repeatedly called upon to temper his wife's enthusiasm in the matter of costs. At the same time, the Brunners were delighted to pay for the very best medical support for Shelagh during her confinement and when the baby was born, the eminent Court physician, Lord Dawson of Penn, was in attendance. A few weeks earlier he had delivered the future Queen Elizabeth into the world.

In preparation for the move to London, a skeleton staff was retained at Belmont Hall whilst several key personnel transferred to Roehampton Court, including Thomas Holdstock and his wife and Harold Dorrington. Holdstock had worked for the Brunners from 1913 and enjoyed what may best be described as a privileged, but fiery, relationship with Ethel Brunner to whom he was principally engaged as personal chauffeur. In the servants' quarters at Belmont Hall, the gossips said that if anyone knew how to handle their temperamental mistress, it was Holdstock. She had fired him on many occasions, only to instantly reinstate him and then advance him money in lieu of wages, apparently to offset his all too frequent impecunious circumstances.

At Green Cottage, the domestic arrangements suited Ethel Brunner admirably. She was able to look after the baby, attend to the refurbishment of Roehampton Court, organise fund-raising for the Spahlinger tuburculosis clinic and indulge in her writing. It was a situation which she happily envisaged would continue until Christmas. Meanwhile, Roscoe Brunner, still reluctant to wholly sever himself from the umbilical cord of Belmont Hall, had settled into Brunner Mond's company apartment, at the head office, in Cavendish Square, London. Here he was attended by the resident steward, William Beldan who had been in the employ of Brunner Mond & Company for five years. Occasionally, Brunner did spend weekends with his wife at Green Cottage, but at this time their marriage had become something of a convenience and, generally, they both preferred to lead separate lives, although upon completion of Roehampton Court it was their intention to at least put on a public show of marital contentment.

Brunner's weekdays in the city revolved around his gentleman's club, the Bath Club, the former Marquess of Abergavenny's home in Dover Street, and his preparations at Cavendish Square for the new business opportunities which he was eagerly anticipating with Mond's promised British holding company. Certainly by September, he was beginning to find London life far more palatable than he had imagined. Despite the upheavals engulfing Brunner Mond & Company, he was facing the future with renewed vigour.

What he could not possibly have anticipated was the scale of change as Sir Alfred Mond began to rearrange the pieces on his chessboard to form an altogether different pattern. When he had sailed for the Continent, and then the United States, he was scheming an international consortium, but when he returned it was with an entirely different concept, the Aquitania Agreement and a British-only merger of the chemical industry. With his trademark ruthlessness, he had jettisoned the Chemical & Dye Corporation, of America, the Farben Group, of Germany, and, most significantly, the planned holding company, in London.

News of the British merger proposals, made public on Thursday October 21st, 1926, caused a sensation in industrial circles and two days later, the London Times announced that all I.C.I. board appointments were to be left to the discretion of the respective founding companies. So, on Monday October 25th and armed with a first class curriculum vitae and Mond's word, Roscoe Brunner would have been in a buoyant mood as he took his seat at the scheduled monthly board meeting of Brunner Mond, the company he had effectively headed for the best part of twenty years. It was true there had been the unsavoury matter of the Lever Brothers' settlement, but that apart, his business track record had been impeccable and he was eagerly anticipating confirmation of his appointment onto the board of I.C.I.. He must, therefore, have been stunned beyond belief when the names were read out. There were places for Jack Brunner, Sir Alfred's son, Henry, and even J.G.Nicholson, whose reputation had also been badly tarnished in the Lever Brothers' debacle, but not Roscoe Brunner and he was bitterly humiliated. In the clamour of the Aquitania Agreement, he had either been forgotten, or ignored, as Mond's promises had drifted away on the Atlantic breeze.

For Brunner, the most galling aspect would, most certainly, have been the thought that Henry Mond, the johnny-come-lately, the upstart, was to be appointed Labour Director, a position to which he had every right to believe he was considerably more qualified, especially given the universal acclaim that had marked his outstanding record in labour relations with Brunner Mond & Company.

The new directors from Brunner Mond were all hand-picked by Sir Alfred Mond who was now possessed with the supreme power that had continually alluded him in politics. Only in the case of his son was Mond swayed by sentiment, as highlighted by Lloyd George who, commenting upon Sir Alfred's defection from the Liberal Party, once said:

'He did not change his party for his own ends. I think many reasons had been involved, but one of those was because of his own son. One day, not so very long before, Mond asked me to lunch. We talked of the party and he said, 'The prospects are bad'. They certainly were. 'Take my son,' said Mond, 'there is a young fellow with gifts. What does the party hold for him?' I think therein lies one great reason why Mond wished to change and associate himself with a party which would give his son broader scope for a career in politics. I am certain that he did not like the thought of his own son's political career being in the arctic regions of Liberalism. He wanted to transplant the young tree.'

It was not just in politics that father wanted to transplant son. Caught up in the political turmoil and without a Parliamentary seat after 1924, Henry Mond had become inextricably drawn into his father's emerging business dreams. He was the perfect ally and when his father machinated himself into the chairmanship of Brunner Mond & Company, he was at his side and was immediately appointed onto the board. For such a young man, only just twenty-seven when Roscoe Brunner was forced to resign, he soon began to wield immense power for he was the one person Mond genuinely believed that he could trust. It was he who had visited Stanley Baldwin, to test out reaction on the original Anglo-German-American alliance and it was he who first advocated acceptance when Sir Harry McGowan began mooting the idea of creating Imperial Chemical Industries. He was also with the Brunner Mond delegation to meet with the Chemical & Dye Corporation in New York and, with the rest of his father's sycophants, was very much a party to the drawing up of the Aquitania Agreement. They were all imbued with the I.C.I. dream.

Roscoe Brunner's omission from the directorship nominees was a crushing blow and one can readily appreciate why the coroner reasoned that he had been left teetering on the brink of suicide. However, Ingleby Oddie was badly mistaken. It was a spurious assumption which the police would surely have realised had they thoroughly investigated Roscoe and Ethel Brunner's behaviour and movements in the days immediately following the Brunner Mond board meeting.

Far from being suicidal, Roscoe Brunner was in reasonably good heart when he set off, on the following day, to visit Cheshire, initially to chair a minor meeting of Brunner Mond directors and then to attend a dinner of the Northwich Conservative Association at which he was to be the principal guest speaker. A new recruit to the Conservative ranks, Brunner received a rapturous welcome when he rose to propose the evening's first toast and the local newspaper described him as being in 'fine form', the reporter noting that he appeared 'radiantly happy' and that '...no director of the large chemical firm of Brunner Mond is held in greater respect by the workforce who idolize him'.

The newspaper also printed at great length a speech in which he complimented the Conservative Government and outlined why he had recently decided to forsake the Liberal Party. Several hundred guests were present, including a number of fellow Brunner Mond directors, and not the slightest hint of anguish was detected, even though the I.C.I. merger was a major topic of conversation following publication that morning of a detailed list of the new company's directors.

The local newspaper commented: 'It is a very great disappointment locally that he (Roscoe Brunner) is not on the new board...'.

Maybe, Brunner, inwardly tormented over his omission from the I.C.I. board, was putting on a brave face, making the best of a sorry affair, but what of his wife in London? How was this impulsive, highly-strung woman managing to maintain her self control?

She would have been acutely aware of the situation and yet, totally out of character, and on the face of it quite inexplicably, she did not immediately react and nor did she make any attempt to contact the newspapers until eight days later. What was she waiting for? What were they both waiting for? It should have been a crucial line of inquiry, but as neither the police, nor the coroner, thought it necessary to seek an explanation, they missed a further prognosis with which to utterly repudiate their own jaundiced view of the tragedy.

The jigsaw only begins to fall into place when we consider the true fulcrum of this tragedy... and it had, literally, been under the detectives' noses from the very start. It concerned the widely-reported announcement that the Marquess of Reading (Rufus Isaacs) had been appointed a director of Imperial Chemical Industries, the magnitude of which simply cannot be over-estimated, occurring as it did precisely on the day that Ethel Brunner commenced her round of visits to the newspaper offices. It was also, crucially, the day upon which she apparently gave vent to her anger at Sir Alfred Mond's home in Lowndes Square, London, where an unsavoury doorstep altercation took place. Mond was probably not at home, but in a state of high dudgeon, it seems Ethel Brunner made some serious accusations and threats concerning the proposed merger.

Mond, Beau Mond of the Cambridge undergraduates, desperate to keep the I.C.I. merger from being derailed as, like some out-of-control express, it rushed towards its destiny, was engaged in the greatest poker game of his life and in his deck of cards Roscoe Brunner hardly ranked above the deuce. Mond was a frustrated statesman who wanted the world, or at least the British Empire, and possessed with immense self-confidence and immense wealth he was well suited to belong to that breed of powerful men who are capable of disdainfully obliterating from their minds the mundane and the inconsequential. In the ferment of merger, Roscoe Brunner had become just such an inconsequence.

At the Brunner Mond board meeting, on Monday October 25th, Mond had announced the names of twelve founding I.C.I. directors, all of them from the merging companies. However, he and McGowan each had a further appointment to make. McGowan chose John Rogers, on behalf of Nobel Industries, and Mond, cunningly procastinating, had certainly led Roscoe Brunner to believe that he would be the final Brunner Mond nomination. Why else had Brunner set off for

Cheshire in such reasonably good heart, to attend the Conservative Association dinner, and what other explanation can there be for Ethel Brunner not immediately commencing her forays to the newspapers?

The answer is clear - they were obviously anticipating formal confirmation.

It never arrived for, Mond was favouring others. 'I want men like Reading, Colwyn and Weir for my directors,' he had said privately... and Reading was to be his choice, not Roscoe Brunner.

Mond and Reading, the former Viceroy of India, were close political allies and enjoyed a deep personal friendship bonded by the marriage of Mond's eldest daughter, Eva, to Reading's son Gerald Isaacs (Viscount Erleigh). They were both barristers, former Liberal MPs, financiers of the first calibre, and early staunch supporters of Lloyd George. As Rufus Isaacs, Lord Reading entered Parliament in 1904 and later he became Attorney General, notably prosecuting Emmeline Pankhurst at the height of the militant suffragette disturbances. Whilst serving as Attorney General he was also caught up in the sensational Marconi scandal which involved his brother, Godfrey Isaacs, who was managing director of the Marconi Wireless and Telegraph Company. It was alleged that Rufus Isaacs, in conspiracy with other high-ranking Liberal politicians, including Lloyd George, had sought to make share profits by exercising unfair influence to ensure that Marconi won a contract to provide the Post Office with a long-distance service. In spite of these revelations and the ensuing political furore, Rufus Isaacs' progress was not hindered and from 1913-21 he was Lord Chief Justice of England, an office from which he presided over the famous treason trial of the Irishman, Roger Casement. During the war he served as Special Ambassador and High Commissioner to the USA and,

Green Cottage, Roehampton.

afterwards, was appointed Viceroy of India, a regal post to which it was said he was selected because he was a Jew, '...being in a sense Oriental and therefore having a natural bond with the Indian people'. He served five years as Viceroy, the most powerful position in the British Empire, and returned to England to be created a Marquess. By coincidence, Lord Reading's departure from India was reported in the London Times in January 1926, on the same page as Mond's resignation from the Liberal Party. The writing was, indeed, on the wall!

Mond had always held Reading in the highest regard, considering him an important and calming influence on Lloyd George and when he left to become Viceroy, Mond had correctly predicted the Prime Minister's downfall. He had said: 'Directly Reading's calming influence is withdrawn from him his power will decline.' During his own, temporary, demise from the House of Commons, Mond had spent an Indian summer with Lord Reading and it was during the return voyage to England that he had begun to formulate his private plans for a powerful and personal takeover of Brunner Mond & Company.

Now publicly, and excelling in his reputation of possessing the knack of chopping off the head of an opponent with an undisturbed air of smiling benevolence, Mond, in handing the last directorship to Reading, had committed the final betrayal. Twice before he had reneged on his promises to Roscoe Brunner; first in offering his support during the Lever troubles and then over his pledge to appoint him as a senior director with the much-vaunted British holding company which then came to be unceremoniously dumped in a New York trash can.

Roehampton Court.

CHAPTER FIFTEEN
MOND'S ROLE IN THE WAR

A ll men have secrets and those in public life have more reason than most to ensure that the skeletons remain firmly locked in the cupboard. Sir Alfred Mond was no exception. For all his undoubted talents, and his enormous generosity as a public benefactor, he had been involved in some obscure businesss dealings and, during his political career, too many unexplained and controversial occurances.

By far the most important of these concerned his role in the First World War, when not a single individual in all of Britain raised the emotions more than he. Fanaticism against Germans and German Jews was widespread during the war and any name without the sweet tang of the English countryside was suspect, particularly that of a leading politician and, later, a Government Minister.

At the outbreak of hostilities it was alleged that when Germany had been preparing for its assault on Europe it had honeycombed the countries it sought to destroy with spies and secret influences, financed from Berlin, the 'hidden hand', and one London magazine demanded that the Government take immediate action, at the highest level, by publishing a 'list of all men of German stock, or of Hebrew stock, who have received distinctions, honours, titles, appointments, contracts or sinecures, both inside or outside the House of Commons, Lords and Privy Council'.

Neither the Government, nor millitary intelligence, would be drawn, although in Mond's case his German connections were well known and whatever he subsequently achieved as a politician, he was mistrusted and bitter recriminations were awaiting him. In fact, the outcry reached a crescendo as the war in France stumbled to its bitter conclusion and it centred upon his dealings as chairman of the Mond Nickel Company, an offshoot of the Mond Trust which had originated through his father in 1881 at the formation of Brunner Mond as a limited company.

Following his father's death, Mond had set about reconstruction, the old company giving way to new in July 1914. Dealing in 'nickel, copper and other metals', Mond Nickel had always relied heavily on trading through Germany and Austria and held upwards of a dozen important patents in the two countries. Furthermore, the established policy was to sell its refined products only through Henry Merton & Co., a subsidiary of the German Metal Combination, based in Frankfurt, and despite the war this arrangement had continued until well into 1915. Yet whilst other British companies were facing summary trial in the criminal courts, Mond Nickel, headed by one of the country's leading politicians, escaped investigation, let alone prosecution. That was bad enough, but Mond Nickel's misdemeanours went further following the announcement that all existing shareholders of the pre-1914 company were to receive an equivalent allotment of shares in the restructured business, the only proviso being that formal acceptance was to be in writing within thirty days. However, the terms of this agreement, filed with Somerset House on July 31st, 1914, were quickly overtaken by the world crisis and a King's Proclamation 'Trading with the Enemy', the provisions of which included the following:

From and after the date of this Proclamation (September 9th, 1914) the following prohibitions shall have effect...and we hereby accordingly warn all persons carrying on business or being in our Dominions... (5) Not to enter into any transaction or complete any transaction already entered into with an enemy in any stocks, shares or other securities.

Remarkably, Mond Nickel ignored the notice and in late September, and with the country awash with talk of war and his own credibility and patriotism called into question, Sir Alfred Mond formally sanctioned the allotment of three-hundred preference shares to his cousin, Dr Richard Mond, whose address was listed as Holzdamm No.36 Hamburg. At the same time, and in further breach of the King's Proclamation, negotiations and share transactions had continued with other German citizens and businesses whose names were formally registered at Somerset House.

These were: Ernest Wertheimer, Frankfurt; Otto Hirsh, Frankfurt; W.M.Heinrich, Leipzig; the Dresden Bank; Clara Hahn, Holstein, Prussia; Dr Ludwig Mathais, Berlin; Emma Wuth, Munich; Louisa Cannell, Munich; Marie Altsmann, Wiesbaden; Herbert Leer, Hamburg; Herbert & Anna Winkler, Berlin; Emmy Leer, Bonn.

The combined holding actually amounted to only 17,775 shares, about one per cent of the total ownership of the restructured company, but it was the principle of the action, not the quantity that was important. Mond had always held the view that 'the businessmen of both countries should exercise their undoubted right to tell politicians and diplomats that a way must and shall be found to make a reality of our mutual desire for friendly relations' and, anyway, the wartime restrictions afforded him absolute immunity. Be that as it may, he was a clear-headed businessmen, a barrister and a serving MP who could not possibly have failed to realise, without the necessity of legislation, that share transactions between British and German residents during wartime was not only illegal, but downright unpatriotic.

Finally, in 1918 and with the war over, Mond's accusers saw the chance to resurrect the affair and open old wounds, especially as he had become a serving Minister in the Coalition Government. They called for his resignation, or his dismissal, and when neither was forthcoming they claimed it was because of his vast financial support for Lloyd George. One publication, the 'New Witness', rounded viciously on the First Commissioner of Works with a scathing attack by its Editor, the author, G.K.Chesterton. The object of Chesterton's newspaper, it was said, was to make the public aware of political corruption and government by the wealthy, plutocrats of the ilk of Sir Alfred Mond.

> The case of Alfred Mond is particularly grave, and whatever view may be taken as to the culpability of his co-directors, he at least should be arraigned before a British jury. The Trading with Enemy Amendment Act, November 27th, 1914, provides that every director, manager, secretary, or other officer of a company who is knowingly a party to trading with the enemy as prohibited inter alia by Proclamation 2 of 1914 shall be liable to the punishment provided, which in the event of arraignment may be penal servitude for seven years and cannot be less than such servitude for three years.

The following week Chesterton took on the entire British Establishment for what he said was its 'appalling conspiracy of silence' in the affair:

> The most remarkable thing that has happened in connection with Sir Alfred Moritz Mond since we published the truth concerning the Mond Nickel Co. is that, to all appearance, nothing has happened. We have no communication from Mond or anyone representing him: we believe that he is still a Minister of the Crown. The Prime Minister has not answered our challenge, nor has anyone questioned him on the subject. Finally, and most significant of all, there had not, so far as we know, appeared anywhere in the official Press so much as a reference to the astounding facts which we have disclosed...

It might have been thought that Harmsworth with his supposed ferocity towards the foreigner and his much advertised determination to eradicate every trace of German influence, would have taken the matter up. But his hundred megaphonic organs, from The Times to the Girl's Best Friend, are silent on the topic. It might be thought the Press which professes to be 'in opposition', the Chronicle, the News, the Star, and even Mond's whilom organ the Westminster Gazette, which he abandoned (after the Mond Nickel transactions) on account of his sudden conversion to the desirability of Conscription, would draw attention to the curious inconsistency between the professions of the Government and the acts of one of its members. But they are silent...

Ever since the war began the mass of patriotic men have been conscious of an impersonal and omnipresent power strangling the patriotic action of the nation and weakening its enormous effort against the enemy. The feeling has been a spontaneous one, provoked by a thousand inexplicable actions and inactions on the part of the group that governs us...

Let us take a concrete instance. Tribitsch 'Lincoln' was admittedly a German spy. He was a Member of Parliament. But why was he a Member of Parliament? Was it because the hardy northern working men whom he was supposed to represent cried out with one voice: 'Only an Austrian Jew can properly express our aspirations'? We think not. 'Lincoln' was 'sent down' with the Machine and its money behind him. Why was he sent down? Presumably because somebody who had a pull on the Machine wanted him to be in Parliament - from motives into which it is hardly necessary to inquire. Who that somebody was we cannot know for certain while the Funds are a secret. We do not know whether Krupps subscribed to these funds. We do not know whether William II. subscribed. The presumption is that they did, directly or indirectly, for it was an obvious prudent and profitable thing for them to do and there was absolutely no human power to check them in doing it. But we do not know. There is one thing, however, that we do know. We know with a moral certitude of one man who subscribed lavishly first to the old Party Funds and later to the new Fund created to float the Mr George Government on its patriotic course. That man is Alfred Moritz Mond.

'There is a real reason for emphasising this fact alongside of the crime of which Mond stands accused. It is not merely that the money which financed the politicians came from ventures like the Mond Nickel Co., from the subscriptions of men like W.M.Heinrich, of Liepsig, Otto Hirsh, of Frankfurt, and Herbert Brandholt, from Berlin, with whom Mond continued his financial transactions in defiance of the Government proclamation long after the war had been declared. It is that the immunity which this man enjoyed and still enjoys not only from administrative action but from criticism in any section of the press is plainly due to the use he has made of his money in buying such immunity from the politicians... And now this man stands accused on the plain testimony of public documents of having carried through financial transactions with Germans in Germany, after and in defiance of the King's proclamation - that is to say of treason...

(Tribitsch Lincoln was a naturalised alien, described by the Sunday Times as 'the country's most relentless conman'. In turn, he was a thief, a missionary in Canada, a curate in Kent, a Liberal MP and a wartime double agent for Britain and Germany.)

Critics often perceived an unpleasant streak of anti-Semitism in Chesterton's views, but few could argue that his stance over Mond's immunity was not vindicated. The authorities remained steadfast and not a single criminal charge was ever levelled against Mond who, characteristically, remained aloof, unmoved and apparently untainted by the gathering tumult. As Chesterton had correctly predicted, the mainstream British press, with a few exceptions, chose to ignore the clamour and in the end it was left to the actions of a resolute London barrister, Percival F. Smith, to bring prominence to the case. He commenced by writing an article, 'Our Gold Lords', in which he demanded exposure of Mond's treachery:

> There can be no doubt whatever that the Mond Nickel Co. had been guilty of the crime of trading with the enemy, and the facts show a strong presumptive case against Alfred Mond, His Majesty's First Commissioner of Works. That individual may be able to prove that, though the chairman of the company when the crime was committed, he did not know of the allotment of shares or of any transaction in connection therewith after the outbreak of War. But the onus of such proof rests upon him, and here an immediate demand is made that he be put on trial.

Still with no sign of criminal proceedings against Mond, Smith followed with a formal complaint to the Director of Public Prosecutions, Sir Charles Matthews, who replied that he was satisfied that no offence had been committed and that the Board of Trade had actually authorised the registration of the Mond Nickel shares. If this was indeed the truth, argued Smith, then the Board of Trade was itself implicated in a cover-up.

Eventually, the growing scandal forced questions in the House of Commons and the Board of Trade had to amend its version of events, stating that the offending share certificates had never, in fact, been sent to the individuals and businesses listed in the Mond Nickel Company allotment of 1914. Furthermore, the 'enemy' shares had actually been vested in the Public Trustee and had subsequently been sold to other parties who were not considered 'enemies' under the King's Proclamation.

Smith was far from placated and he continued his attack by making application to the Bow Street Magistrate, Sir John Dickenson, for the issue of a warrant for the arrest of Sir Alfred Mond, a quite amazing indictment against a Minister of the Crown. The application was thrown out, but at least the national press was left with little alternative but to give the matter prominence, especially when Smith took his plea to the King's Bench Division of the High Court. Again he failed, but this time more on a technicality, the Law Lords ruling that he had been unable to prove conclusively whether or not the Board of Trade had issued a licence to formally allot the Mond Nickel shares to the 'enemy'. In his summing up, Mr Justice Darling made it clear that if the absence of a formal licence could have been shown, there would most certainly have been a requirement to take the matter to trial.

So Smith was foiled, but the matter rumbled on and, at last, the truth was elicited in a further House of Commons' question. Sir Alfred Stanley, President of the Board of Trade, sensationally admitted that his department had not actually considered the allocation of the Mond Nickel Company shares until December 3, 1914, i.e. four months after the outbreak of war. It was an astonishing development and it meant that Sir Alfred Mond and his co-directors had clearly flouted the law by using the delay to negotiate the share transactions with the German citizens. To further add insult to injury, Sir Alfred Stanley also declared that the surplus unallocated 'enemy' shares, i.e. those shares not taken taken up by the German citizens, had only been vested in the Public Trustee that very month, October 1918, and not, as had been inferred, in 1914.

It was a complete about-face and made a nonsense of the Department of Trade's earlier statement. The Financial News dubbed it a 'revelation of political trickery', but as there was no recourse to return directly to law, Smith, Chesterton and the New Witness demanded urgent action from the Attorney General. However, Mond escaped again. His immunity, argued Smith and Chesterton, was in his money and his political power which he had used to deceive the public. At every opportunity they pilloried him, frequently drawing in his association with Brunner Mond & Co. who during the war had felt the need to issue a strongly worded statement in an attempt to rebutt rumours that it was collaborating with Germany.

Finally, on the eve of the 1918 General Election, at a public meeting in Swansea, Percival Smith openly accused Mond of being a traitor and a liar. There could have been no greater insult to Mond and though he ultimately pursued a number of individuals for libel and slander, he would not be drawn into a court action against Smith and Chesterton who were certainly not alone in clamouring for his political head. Indeed, whenever during the war the question of 'enemy agents' had arisen, Mond's name always seemed to the fore, not least as a consequence of a claims in a book by the self-styled spy-buster William Le Queux who suspected that German spies and sympathisers had infiltrated the highest positions of the British Government, a charge dismissed by the authorities as sheer fantasy.

After the war, and having escaped punishment over the Mond Nickel share dealings, Mond, of course, went on to attain even higher government office as Minister of Health. The case against him had never been proved, but then he had never been brought to criminal trial for, as is often the case in matters of litigation, wealth and influence so often over-rides justice. If nothing else, the official lack of action served to spur his detractors and in Swansea his political opponents were determined to expose him.

Accursed as being a 'German Jew', he was regarded by members of the local Conservative and Unionist Association as '...not being a fit and proper person to represent any British constituency in the Imperial Parliament', and they passed a formal resolution stating just that. They also published an announcement in a Welsh national newspaper stating that Mond was a hypocrite and, with his dual loyalties, a pro-German influence in the House of Commons who would weaken Great Britain's resolve to exact the fullest terms of war reparation. This was, in fact, absurd. Mond was one of the strongest advocates for enforcing strict terms on the Germans, but the scene was set in Swansea for the ugliest, wildest election battle of his tempestuous political career, especially when a fellow Liberal declared in the House of Commons that 'Free Trade chemical manufacturers like the Hon. Member for Swansea had been bleeding the country all through the war'.

Through it all Mond simply smiled. He had been a target during the anti-German hysteria of the war years and now, in Peace, he considered he was being subjected to the grubbiest form of political sleaze. He was still smiling when the electorate of Swansea sent him back victorious to Westminster, although his celebrations did not last, for in the Spring of 1919 he was literally goaded into the civil courts by the Silver Badge Party, a London-based amalgam of ex-officers and men of HM Forces. These military veterans, frustrated by what they saw as an outrageous political cover-up over the Mond Nickel share dealings, were determined to draw Mond's thunder and in a well-publicised operation they began displaying inflammatory notices throughout the capital, stating: 'Sir Alfred Mond is a traitor; he allotted shares to Huns during the war'.

A photograph of one of the posters, with a large crowd gathered around it in Charing Cross, appeared in the Daily Graphic and Mond immediately slapped a High Court injunction on the miscreants. The writ was ignored and as a consequence the matter was laid before a special jury of the High Court Chancery Division headed by Mr Justice Darling, a former Member of Parliament for Deptford and one of the Law Lords who had rejected Smith's earlier plea to bring Mond to justice.

What followed was three days of pure theatre, or perhaps 'pure farce' would be a better analogy, between self-representing defendants and Mond's army of powerful counsel led by his former War Cabinet colleague, the venomous Ulsterman, Sir Edward Carson K.C., a one-time Attorney General.

In the civil courts British justice is a lie. The only truth is money and whatever we are supposed to believe about each man's inane right to defend himself, barrack-room lawyering is abhorrent to the judiciary, especially at the exalted level of the High Courts. Reports of the proceedings make it plain that the defendants were treated throughout with patronising contempt by Mr Justice Darling, who certainly lived up to his criminal court reputation of being a 'hanging judge'. In this case he simply allowed the defendants enough proverbial rope to hang themselves. The British Establishment was not really interested in

142

Mond's supposed crime; the principle at stake was whether two eccentric individuals, Harry McLeod Fraser and Henry Hamilton Beamish, on behalf of the Silver Badge Party, should be allowed to buck the legal system and bring to task a Minister of the Crown. If they were successful it would set a dangerous precedent for every lunatic who ever held a grudge against a member of the government.

The case hinged simply upon the defendants' ability to demonstrate positively that Mond was a traitor, therefore validating the words on the offending poster which had, specifically, been displayed at the home of Fraser who had acted in association with Beamish. Sir Edward Carson stated that an original poster, displayed in the window of the house-cum-headquarters of the Silver Badge Party, in Spring Gardens, Charing Cross, had been removed following the original injunction, but this had been instantly replaced with a reproduction page from the Daily Graphic and also a copy of Mond's writ.

The words 'He is a traitor' had been underlined in red ink and chalked alongside was the phrase: 'He now squirms'. Later an additional notice was erected, stating: 'Mond first of all tried to get the police to make us take this notice down. His next move was to bring pressure to bear upon the landlord to turn us out, but we hope we have frustrated this move. It is now up to Mond to take action in the courts. Has he the courage to do it?'

Mond certainly did not lack courage, just as long as he had at his back the finest legal brains that money could buy and he protested his innocence throughout. The posters were false and maliciously published; moreover he was not aware of the Mond Nickel Company's share allocation to the Germans during the period October 26 - December 8, 1914.

This was an amazing admission for a chairman such as Mond who ran his companies with the zeal of a dictator. It was true that in the general workings of his business and political affairs he would often become impatient over trivial detail, but on the other hand he was a trained barrister and the intricate detail, the small print, would seldom miss his personal scrutiny, particularly when there might have followed ramifications of a legal nature. It was also impossible for anyone acquainted with Mond to genuinely believe that he did not know what was going on over the Mond Nickel share dealings as, after all, some of the shares were being allotted to his own relatives in Germany.

Under cross examination by Sir Edward Carson, Fraser said he was the honorary secretary of the Silver Badge Party and he considered Mond to be a traitor in that he had offended against a trust. He was a Member of Parliament and had broken the provisions of the Trading with Enemy Act. Beamish, a newspaper publisher was next to the witness stand. He said that he had been described as conspirator, but it was untrue. His own father had been an admiral, a one-time A.D.C. to Queen Victoria and he personally had served in the Boer War, India and Ceylon. Prior to the proceedings he had never seen Mond, but he knew him to be an international Jewish financier who was out to destroy Great Britain. Beamish maintained he was not anti-Semite, but he was an anti-corruptionist.

In his defence Beamish then called Henry Gardiner, the chairman of Henry Merton and Company, of Germany, with whom Mond Nickel had traded so profusely. Despite a subpoena, Mr Gardiner, perhaps mindful of Sir Alfred's multifarious business associations, failed to appear. Mond's own case was supported by one of his closest political allies, Lord Moulton, the Minister of Munitions, who testified as to his 'loyal and patriotic character', notably in the way in which he had immediately placed Brunner Mond on an all-out war footing in 1915.

'This country could not have maintained the war without nitrate of ammonia supplied by Brunner Mond & Company, ' stated Lord Moulton. 'They devised methods, erected factories, and exerted themselves to the utmost and nothing could have been better than their work.'

Justice Darling - Did they know whom you were blowing to pieces?

Lord Moulton - Yes; they materially assisted the country against the enemy.

Lord Moulton was absolutely correct in his summary of Brunner Mond's role in the war, but how much of it was actually due to Sir Alfred Mond was highly questionable. The company had provided around eighty per cent of Britain's explosives and, not unreasonably, it made a handsome profit into the bargain, but by the time of some of the bloodiest battles, Mond had already relinquished his directorship in favour of government office and as his biographer later admitted: '...as a Minister he had neither authority over nor responsibility for the activities of Messrs Brunner Mond and Co.'.

Mond had not been slow to take the credit, but the gratitude of the nation was more rightly due to Roscoe Brunner and his lieutenants who had guided the company's vital work throughout the war.

Mond's old antagonist, the London barrister, Percival F. Smith, spoke for Fraser. He maintained that the records of the Mond Nickel Company showed Mond to have attended board meetings in August and December 1914, when the enemy share allotments had been made to the German citizens and organisations and it was therefore ridiculous to suggest that he was not in receipt of the information. Mond countered that he knew nothing of the share dealings and, as chairman of the Mond Nickel Company, it was not his duty to see that the share register was properly kept. Besides, there were 4,200 shareholders in the company of which only thirteen were considered enemies. He also insisted that, depending upon circumstances, any man who had knowingly traded with the enemy during wartime would have been guilty of committing a 'disgraceful scandal' and would have deserved to have been taken out and shot!

With Mr Justice Darling's patience beginning to wear decidedly thin it was the turning point in the case. When Beamish tried to bring out what he termed Mond's 'treacherous role' on the Balfour Committee, dealing with the country's finance and trade, Mr Justice Darling, whom it was often said allowed himself to behave with a levity quite unsuitable to a courtroom, interceded: 'What has struck me about that committee is that it did much more business in a shorter time than would be possible in this court...'

And when Beamish attempted to draw in the interminable Brunner Mond versus Lever Brothers legal wranglings, he was further rebuked by His Lordship:

'Really, I don't know. I suppose it is going to be contended that if a person uses soap he is a traitor.'

Beamish's meanderings knew no bounds and in one instance Mond was asked if he had heard the name of Gaby Deslys and was he, Mond, being of German stock, out to destroy the character and undermine the moral constitution of the British people.

His Lordship - I think I caught the name of Gaby Deslys. Is that a man or a woman?

Mond - She is a French actress.

His Lordship - Oh! I thought perhaps it might be a German propagandist.

Next, Mond's involvement with the English Review magazine was brought into question since, at one time, he had helped to finance the venture, as well as the Westminster Gazette. Beamish read out certain passages from the English Review, contending that the words used demonstrated the publication's immorality.

Sir Edward Carson - I find in one of the volumes of the English Review a poem by your Lordship. It is in Volume 9, and entitled 'In the Abbey'.

His Lordship - Now, Sir Edward, as a poem by myself has been named as appearing in the English Review, which is the subject of denunciation by Mr Beamish, I will ask you to read it out.

Sir Edward, one of the most learned counsel in England, did as he was bid and, fittingly, it brought the charade of cross-examination to a close. All that remained was the summing up in which Sir Edward spun an additional protective web of legalese around Mond.

Through their well-intentioned but bungling efforts, and pitched as they were against a battery of formidable counsel, Messrs Fraser and Beamish only succeeded in destroying the entire credibility of whatever case existed against Mond and no criminal court, or civil one for that matter, would ever again be disposed to consider the charges. There was little alternative but for the jury to find in Mond's favour, Judge Darling awarding him the substantial sum of £5,000 damages.

In the midst of the legal technicalities and adjournments leading to the actual case in London, Mond and his entire legal team set out for Cardiff to fight a second, and potentially more serious libel action. The defendants before Mr Justice Lush and the Glamorgan Assizes were the South Wales Post and its Editor, a former Mayor of Swansea, Mr David Davies, who stood jointly accused of publishing libellous speeches against Mond during the 1918 General Election campaign in Swansea. The passages complained of included the sentence: 'We Welshman have not the adaptability of men like Sir Alfred Mond. We cannot take our nationality on and off like a coat.'

Another was: 'At the Peace Conference and in the diplomacy which follows the war, we do not want any dual loyalty.'

Within the context of fierce electioneering both statements appeared rather innocuous and it seemed perfectly reasonable for the newspaper to claim 'fair comment' on matters of public interest. Sir Edward Carson did not agree, arguing that the allegations against Mond were being used as a stick with which to beat him. The words implied that Mond was a hypocrite and that he was using his influence on behalf of Germany. No more cruel charge could be made, and if it were true, Mond ought to be turned out of office. Further allegations concerned Mond's alleged attempts to supply Germany through Norway and Sweden during the war. This was also a 'foul lie', insisted Sir Edward.

In the witness box during a five-hour grilling, Mond produced his birth certificate to show that he was a British citizen and he denied what he termed 'terrible accusations' in which it was claimed he had been sent to the House of Commons as a German agent.

Lord Moulton's evidence on Brunner Mond's war efforts was again helpful and when asked about Sir Alfred Mond's loyalty, he said:

'He was doing his best for his country, as were all the directors of Brunner Mond & Company. It was so deliberately the policy of the company that the directors had not to be even formally consulted when it was wanted. It was done as a matter of course.'

In fact, Lord Moulton's evidence, strictly confined to Brunner Mond's involvement in the war and the work of Dr Ludwig Mond, was all that was offered to support Mond. He did not need more for Davies and the newspaper withdrew, unreservedly, and formally apologised for the allegations. Damages were awarded to Mond.

That was the end, as far as they went, of the legal actions. Mond's name had been cleared although the stigma never fully left him in the eyes of his opponents and many fresh allegations surfaced, but none could ever be substantiated. The arguments in the London trial had specifically centred upon the Mond Nickel Company's allotment of shares to the enemy and Mond's critics whispered that his skin had only been saved by Lloyd George's behind-the-scenes intervention, since his own wife was a registered shareholder of the Mond Nickel Company. In Wales, Davies and the South Wales Post's problem was trying to vindicate charges when the opportunities for Mond may have simply melted away.

Sir Alfred Mond with Lloyd George and Asquith.
Right: Sir Edward Carson.

CHAPTER SIXTEEN

SYMBOL OF MALEVOLENCE

The First World War had reached its shattering climax with Britain and France teetering on the brink of defeat in the spring of 1918 and it is a matter of history that out of adversity the Allies had turned the German offensive and burst through the Hindenburg Line to victory. But what if it had not been so? What if Britain had been left to sue for peace with France broken? Who would have taken on the mantle of the British leader? Certainly not Lloyd George, Asquith, Bonar Law, Curzon or Churchill. It would have required a high-ranking politician with sympathies towards Germany and, whatever his indignation, it may not have been so fanciful of the likes of Percival Smith, Beamish and the others to believe that Sir Alfred Mond, the visionary, the opportunist, might have seen himself as the man for the moment.

Neither as a public benefactor, nor as a political achiever, was Mond ever again fully accepted by the British people. He may have won handsomely in the courts of London and Cardiff, but the charges and his German origins he could never erase. True to character, he was unswerving in his defiance and if he had knowingly traded with the enemy, or indeed acted in some capacity as a German agent, he never once allowed his patriotism to falter in the face of the onslaught. Indeed, he succeeded in walking a tightrope that few men have safely negotiated on their journey through politics when such unabated scandal threatens to engulf them. The London and Cardiff cases were private civil actions, brought by Mond himself, and as far as can be ascertained, he was never investigated by the military intelligence. Officially, Sir Alfred Mond was a loyal British subject and yet, to millions of Britons engaged in the titanic struggle of the First World War, he was despised as an MP, his German sympathies well known.

Puerile xenophobia was rife in every corner of the land and never did it surface more than in London on the night of January 19th, 1917. Silvertown Works, covering an area of about 52,000 square yards of London's dockland, was one of two Brunner Mond factories engaged in purifying massive quantities of T.N.T. for urgent dispatch to the Front. The works were situated at Crescent Wharf and ran parallel with the Great Eastern Railway, with the River Thames on one side and the heavily populated North Woolwich Road on the other. Shortly before seven o'clock, the T.N.T. purifying plant erupted into a ball of fire and within minutes an earth-shattering explosion rocked buildings across the entire city, bringing terror not only to those living in the immediate vicinity of the Brunner Mond works, but also to the townspeople and villagers of southern England who witnessed with horror the flaming night-sky over London. As far away as King's Lynn and Grantham there were reports of minor tremors from the blast and the feeling was widespread that the capital was under attack.

The carnage was unbelievable as practically every individual caught within two-hundred yards of the plant perished. When they finally totalled the casualty list, there were 73 dead and 436 injured. In addition, upwards of 600 people were treated for minor cuts and bruises. Adjoining factories, an oil depot, a gasworks and hundreds of houses were either razed to the ground, or seriously damaged. The only saving grace, if any could be found amidst such wholesale devastation, was that being Saturday evening, T.N.T. purification at the plant had ceased shortly before the fire and only a limited night shift was on duty. Normally, 286 people were employed at the works.

Wartime restrictions prevented the newspapers from pinpointing the exact location of the disaster and an official statement was not issued until almost twenty-four hours later. This all fuelled speculation that the Hun were literally on the doorstep and the Daily Mail later reported:

> The munitions factory simply ceased to exist. Tons of iron were hurled about like feathers. One may see the remains of great boilers, far from where they were fixed, bent like old milk churns, and great pieces of sheet iron, weighing two or

three tons, twisted and torn in shreds. A hole one hundred yards across and eighty feet deep marks the spot where the explosives store once existed. Masses of earth and iron and all sorts of wreckage cover an area of about six acres round. Within that area destruction was absolutely complete. Outside it is as if there had been an earthquake. Houses are roofless and broken. Walls half a mile away were blown down.

Every ambulance and fire engine in London raced to the scene, motor omnibuses and tugs were used to transport the injured. Hospitals were soon overflowing with the injured and makeshift mortuaries with the dead. On the Saturday, the Prime Minister and the Home Secretary visited the scene and an immediate Government inquiry was ordered, under the direction of Sir Ernley Blackwell. Over forty witnesses were subsequently examined, including surviving workers, Brunner Mond's experts and Sir Alfred Mond's friend Lord Moulton, the then Director General of Explosive Supplies, who outlined the background to the creation of the T.N.T. purifying process at Silvertown which, he said, had been of paramount importance in the national interest. Lord Moulton told the inquiry:

'Early in the year 1915 we found our capacity for purifying T.N.T insufficient for the probable task which would be thrown upon it. I had come to the conclusion that I would not allow the makers of T.N.T. to set up purifying works in their factories. The dangers of making T.N.T. are comparatively small, and are of a totally different type to the dangers from purifying and I felt convinced that in order to protect my output I ought not to allow purifying works to be put up in the same place as manufacturing works...

'I heard that these works at Silvertown were standing idle, and that they were the only works which we knew of which were capable of being adapted to a method of purification... a method of washing in hot alcohol. Accordingly we communicated with Messrs Brunner Mond and put the works into their hands, as our agents to adapt them to the process of purification. They have turned out about ten tons a day... I wish to make it plain the part played by Brunner Mond & Co. in this matter. It was we who employed them to let us have these disused works, and we who employed them to adapt them to the new use and to carry it on.'

The inquiry's findings as to the cause of the explosion were generally inconclusive, other than that fire in the melt room of the T.N.T. plant had sparked the catastrophe. The official report stated: 'While it has been clearly established that the explosion followed upon an outbreak of the fire in or above the melt pot, no direct evidence is available to enable us to determine definitely the originating cause of the fire.' The inquiry therefore looked at three possible alternatives - fire by accident; fire by spontaneous ignition and fire produced by a malicious act. As to the latter, the Blackwell Report concluded:

'Careful investigation by the police and other authorities has so far failed to discover any direct evidence that this disaster was maliciously caused. The character and antecedents of all employees at Messrs Brunner Mond's factory have been gone into, and no suspicions attaches to any one of them. We are satisfied that it is the highest degree improbable that any unauthorised person was or could have been upon the premises on the night in question. Nevertheless, the possibility that the disaster was in some way due to enemy agents cannot in the circumstances be overlooked. We know that elsewhere, and especially in the United States, the activities of enemy agents have been directed to interference with the munitions supply of the Allies... It is obvious that the enemy would be attracted by the project of blowing up a T.N.T. factory situated in a populous part of the East End of London. To achieve this object, it is by no means necessary that they should have an agent upon the spot or in the factory itself.'

In the weeks following the incident two Government agents were called on to make discreet visits to the East End to establish whether there was any evidence to support the popular theory that the explosion was, indeed, due to enemy, or pro-German, activity. 'Persons of every class who had no knowledge from whence we came were quite certain that the explosion was not the result of an accident,' said a confidential memorandum to the Blackwell Committee.

'The people are exceedingly loyal in thought and deed. The residents showed great fortitude in spite of their bereavements and loss of employment, but expressed great indignation and feeling against the persons or persons whom they supposed caused the explosion.'

Not one individual stepped forward with the merest hint of proof, but most East Enders were convinced, said the memorandum, that the appalling tragedy was directly related to German spies involved with Brunner Mond & Co., notably Sir Alfred Mond who was, they said, a German.

Justified or not, Mond had again become a symbol of all that was malevolent to the British nation and it was officially recorded that the East Enders had forcibly expressed the view that he should be run out of office or even hanged for treason. Many Brunner Mond employees with rather tenuous foreign links, and even those with foreign-sounding names, were questioned, but Sir Alfred Mond was not amongst them and there the matter was publicly laid to rest, other than the release to the press of a cursory statement on the findings of the Blackwell Inquiry. Obviously the details were never made public in war-stricken Britain and they also remained confidential at the time, two years later, of the libel proceedings involving Mond.

However, there was a footnote. Internal repercussions continued long after the official report as charges of inaccuracies and misleading evidence were levelled at the Blackwell Inquiry, so much so that the Home Secretary, Sir George Cave, was forced to intervene with a sharp rebuke to the critics:

'If the report and recommendations of a committee appointed by the Government to enquire into the causes of a disaster of this character are to be received in this spirit, I am afraid that no-one will in future be willing to undertake such a task, unless indeed he is prepared to produce a report of a purely whitewashing character.'

Whatever the arguments, the single inescapable fact remains that the explosion at Brunner Mond's Silvertown Works caused more damage than all the German air raids on London during the entire war and the incident was never explained to everyone's satisfaction.

Meanwhile, the hatred and mistrust of Mond gathered momentum and yet, remarkably, his political speeches became even more belli-cose.

'I care not what views a man expressed before the war broke out, or what views he is going to express when the war ceases,' he declared. 'I say for God's sake let us all join to win the war, and when we have won it there will be time enough, if we have the inclination, to return to the quarrels of the past. We have to realise the enemy's cunning; there has been too much killing our opponent with the mouth instead of the bullet.'

At the end of the war, more innuendo swept over Mond when a team of technical experts from Brunner Mond received Government permission, from none other than the Minister of Munitions, Lord Moulton, to visit the Haber-Bosch plant in Oppau on the Rhine, in occupied Germany. Whether the visit was pure exploitation or the spoils of victory, it was roundly condemned by the Germans for the Brunner Mond boffins intended to acquire as much detailed informa-tion as possible about the complicated process of synthetically pro-ducing ammonia nitrate for which the Haber-Bosch plant was a pio-neer. Though they were not allowed to sketch or take detailed notes in the plant, the Brunner Mond scientists made a mental note and after-wards in their hotel, secretly committed their findings onto paper. The plan worked well and what they missed on one visit they cleared up the next day. For their return to England, they placed their luggage with their reports and drawings in an armed, locked railway wagon in Germany, but it was mysteriously broken into and plundered. It was thought that someone who knew exactly what the Brunner Mond team was up to had tipped off the Germans.

Again the finger pointed at Mond, but maybe rather ridiculously. The large scale manufacture of nitrogenous fertilisers had long stirred his imagination and he was tremendously excited when Roscoe Brunner bravely instigated the purchase of the former Ministry of Munitions' plant, at Billingham. The largest chemical project of its time and a voracious eater of capital, it was initially a terrifying drain on Brunner Mond's resources, but year upon year, and thanks to Roscoe Brunner's astute chairmanship, it succeeded in increasing its markets and sales and came to be the jewel in the company's crown during the I.C.I. merger negotiations.

At the outset, Brunner Mond had been anxious to share in the Billingham venture with Explosives Trades, the forerunner of Nobel Industries, headed by Sir Harry McGowan, later to become one of the joint founders, with Sir Alfred Mond, of I.C.I, but surprisingly, at the last minute, the explosives company pulled out of the deal. It was a strange twist and Brunner Mond was left alone to single-handedly continue negotiations with Sir Alfred's courtroom ally and friend, Lord Moulton and in the end they bought the plant for a song. (Shortly afterwards, Lord Moulton was appointed chairman of British Dyestuffs Ltd, one of the four companies who were later to merge to form I.C.I..)

Included with the Billingham acquisition was over two hundred and fifty acres of accompanying land which, once safely in Brunner Mond's possession, rather miraculously revealed an unexpected bonus, a thick bed of anhydrite, a form of calcium sulphate, an important basic ingredient in the synthesisation of ammonia.

It was either an incredible stroke of good fortune or a carefully worked ruse and though Brunner Mond and Lord Moulton denied collusion, or any prior knowledge of the existence of the valuable mineral beneath the site, it is difficult to believe that a secret deal was not struck, to the detriment of Nobels. If this had been so, and considering the importance of Billingham in the I.C.I. merger, it may have been information that could have irrevocably damaged the bond between Sir Alfred Mond and Sir Harry McGowan for neither, and it was their one abiding weakness in the crucial weeks between the Aquitania Agreement and the shareholders' ballot, could have hoped to pull off the deal, one without the other.

A crowd gathers to read the Silver Badge Party poster
in Charing Cross.

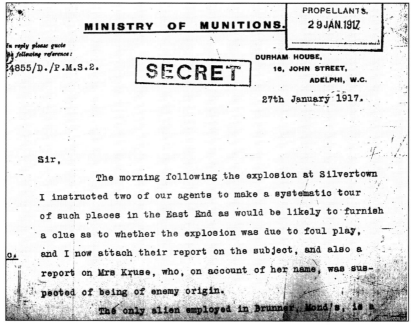

The Blackwell Report into the Silvertown explosion.

CHRONOLOGY OF EVENTS LEADING TO THE
FORMATION OF IMPERIAL CHEMICAL INDUSTRIES

October 1922	Fall of the British Coalition Government.
November 1922	Sir Alfred Mond re-elected Swansea West. Conservative Government elected.
December 1923	Sir Alfred Mond loses Swansea West Parliamentary seat to Lewis Jones (Labour).
December 1923	Sir Alfred Mond rejoins board of directors of Brunner Mond & Company.
January 1924	Sir Alfred Mond visits India to holiday for two months with Viceroy of India, Lord Reading.
March 1924	Roscoe Brunner writes 'letter of confession' to Lever Brothers.
May 1924	Roscoe Brunner re-elected chairman of Brunner Mond & Company.
June 1924	Lever Brothers commence legal action against Brunner Mond & Company.
August 1924	Sir Alfred Mond wins Camarthen by election.
January 1925	Wedding' of Shelagh Brunner and Prince Ferdinand Andreas de Liechtenstein.
May 1925	Roscoe Brunner re-elected chairman of Brunner Mond & Company.
September 1925	Roscoe Brunner falls ill with shingles.
November 1925	Brunner Mond board agrees 'out of court' settlement with Lever Brothers.
January 1926	Sir Alfred Mond resigns Liberal Party.
February 1926	Roscoe Brunner resigns chairmanship of Brunner Mond & Company.
March 1926	Sir Alfred Mond elected acting chairman, Brunner Mond & Co... Roscoe Brunner takes temporary leave from board of directors due to 'ill-health'.
May 1926	Sir Alfred Mond formally elected chairman of Brunner Mond & Company.
June 1926	Roscoe and Ethel Brunner commence move to London.
August 1926	Sir Alfred Mond visits Continent to discuss British/German/American alliance.

September 1926	Sir Alfred Mond meets American Dye Corporation, New York.
October 6, 1926	Sir Alfred Mond abandons talks with Americans, departs USA with McGowan on board S.S.Aquitania.
October 21, 1926	Public announcement of British-only chemical merger, I.C.I..
October 25, 1926	Brunner Mond board confirms I.C.I. directorship nominations. Roscoe Brunner omitted.
October 26, 1926	Roscoe Brunner chairs meeting of Brunner Mond directors.
October 27, 1926	Roscoe Brunner attends Northwich Conservative Association dinner, Cheshire.
November 2, 1926	Public announcement - Lord Reading appointed onto board of I.C.I..Ethel Brunner visits Daily Herald, remonstrates at the home of Sir Alfred Mond. Roscoe Brunner sends to Cheshire for revolver.
November 3, 1926	Ethel Brunner visits Financial News. Deaths of Roscoe and Ethel Brunner at Green Cottage, Roehampton.
November 5,1926	'Imperial Chemical Industries' formally registered. Sir Alfred Mond visits Westminster Coroner.
November 8, 1926	Inquest,Wandsworth, into deaths of Roscoe and Ethel Brunner.
November 9, 1926	Funerals of Roscoe and Ethel Brunner. Sir Alfred Mond submits 'letter of thanks' to Metropolitan Police Commisioner.
November 15, 1926	Letters distributed to shareholders in the merging companies, urging them take up I.C.I shares option.
November 30, 1926	Management of I.C.I. commences.
December 7, 1926	Imperial Chemical Industries incorporated.

IMPERIAL CHEMICAL INDUSTRIES,
LIMITED.

AUTHORISED CAPITAL - £65,000,000

On the assumption that all the shareholders of the participating companies :—

Brunner, Mond and Co., Limited,
Nobel Industries, Limited,
The United Alkali Company, Limited,
British Dyestuffs Corporation, Limited,

exchange their holdings of shares, the issued capital of the new Company on the basis of the exchange will be £56,802,996, divided as follows :—

		£
16,219,306	7 per cent. Cumulative Preference Shares of £1 each (Preferential both as to Capital and Dividends)	16,219,306
31,095,555	Ordinary Shares of £1 each	31,095,555
18,976,270	Deferred Shares of 10s. 0d. each	9,488,135
		£56,802,996

DIRECTORATE :

The first Directors of the new Company are :

The Right Honourable Sir ALFRED MOND, Bart., P.C., M.P. (Chairman).
Sir HARRY McGOWAN, K.B.E. (President and Deputy Chairman).
The Right Honourable The LORD ASHFIELD, P.C.
Sir JOHN BRUNNER, Bart.
G. C. CLAYTON, Esq., C.B.E., M.P.
H. J. MITCHELL, Esq.
HENRY MOND, Esq.
Sir MAX MUSPRATT, Bart.
J. G. NICHOLSON, Esq.
Lt.-Col. G. P. POLLITT, D.S.O.
The Most Honourable The MARQUESS OF READING, P.C., G.C.B., G.C.S.I., G.C.I.E., G.C.V.O.
JOHN ROGERS, Esq., O.B.E.
Sir JOSIAH STAMP, G.B.E.
B. E. TODHUNTER, Esq., O.B.E.

The only director from outside the four merging companies was the Marquess of Reading. His appointment was publicly announced on the day preceding the tragedy at Green Cottage.

CHAPTER SEVENTEEN
THE FINAL DAYS

An eloquent, intelligent and scheming woman, Ethel Brunner almost certainly died because of her own impulsiveness in digressing from a carefully conceived plot. For months she had been in readiness, polishing and perfecting the script according to her husband's roller-coaster business fortunes. The opening chapters had been all Roscoe Brunner's; his paternal management of Brunner Mond & Company, his success as the head of a hugely successful international business and his life in Cheshire. Then followed the return of Sir Alfred Mond, the appalling repercussions of the Lever Brothers' settlement, Brunner's forced resignation and his move to London. It was one story that Ethel Brunner never committed to paper and there remains only disjointed fragments of information, a kaleidoscope of truths and untruths.

Ethel Brunner lived on a knife-edge and when she visited the newspapers she was, like her eponymous heroine Celia, 'trying to manoeuvre things into happening; that she was obsessed with the idea that she would be able to use people; that she never made a friend, or shook hands with a person, except with a view to using them for something'. In sending the final note to the Night Editor of the Daily Herald and promising to write to the Editor of the Financial News, she was clearly preparing the ground for when she would return.

And what could be guaranteed to appeal to a journalist's news-sense more than a scandal involving a Government Minister, whether in office or in retirement? To my mind, and given that a tide of intrigue had been ebbing and flowing beneath the surface ever since his return from politics to industry, there is not the slightest doubt whatsoever about her intentions, or her target... Sir Alfred Mond!

Ethel viewed the I.C.I. merger as odious and contemptible. She believed her husband had been treated shamefully by Mond and his cohorts. She was a woman scorned and this was to be her last, desperate stand to halt the march of merger. Indeed, other than Mond, it is obvious there was nothing else to interest the newspapers.

The sequence of events and the upheavel engulfing the Brunners can be traced, unerringly, to Sir Alfred Mond's return to the board of Brunner Mond, in December, 1923. It is the reason that transcends all others and after the third and final betrayal, i.e. the Lord Reading appointment, she was about to take her revenge.

We cannot know what she intended to reveal, but it is self-evident that to arouse the media's interest she would have required something far more sensational than the emotion-streaked tittle-tattle she had previously conveyed. She was too astute, too familiar with the workings of the press, to have expected anything less and what is more important, before attempting to compromise someone of the public and political standing of Mond, whose track record in the libel courts was already legendary, she would have been fully aware that hard-nosed national journalists would have demanded tangible proof of any alleged scandal involving an ex-Minister. Her word alone would have been insufficient and that being so, is it not reasonable to assume that she must have had in her possession incriminating documents?

It would certainly have been true to character and in keeping with her desire for vengeance against Mond, but more than that, there were compelling clues to indicate just what she was planning.

As mentioned earlier, the general disarray in the writing-room, where the bodies were discovered, was totally overlooked by the police. Documents, letters and, more pointedly, cheque book counterfoils had all been scrutinised, but to Det. Insp. Eve and his team it was an irrelevance, caused by the Brunners themselves. The official file and the statements emphatically show they had not thought through, or connected, Ethel's behaviour in visiting the press with the scene in the writing-room. They were totally unaware that documents, crucial to their inquiry, might have existed, or that Ethel could possibly have paid someone to obtain them.

A monumental error, that was bad enough, but there was still one further decisive piece of evidence and this too was abjectly disregarded. It indicated precisely what Ethel Brunner was planning next. Her hat and coat!

P.C.Whitwell, Dr Nobbs, and the police surgeon, McBride, all reported that she had been wearing a hat and coat at the moment of her death. Yet, the maid, Bella Scott, was adamant in her statement to the police, at the inquest and seventy years later, that when Mrs Brunner arrived at Green Cottage on that evening, her outdoor clothes, including her hat, were placed upon the hall stand.

'I remember taking Mrs Brunner's hat and coat when she came in and she was certainly not wearing them when I took up the tea about half an hour later,' she told me. 'She certainly did not come downstairs again and, anyway, the hat and coat she was wearing when she came in were still on the hall stand.'

Like all women of her day, Ethel Brunner always wore a hat out-doors and, as an integral part of her publicity make-up to promote her novels, she was frequently photographed in some of the most stylish creations. But it was not Ethel Brunner's practice, stressed Bella Scott, to wear a hat indoors... unless she was getting ready to leave the house!

A small but telling observation from a fifteen-year-old girl, this unequivocally shows that the police, either accidently because of their own incompetence, or deliberately because they were under pressure from outside influences, took the investigation down a blind alley. This tragedy was not about what Ethel Brunner had done, nor about what she had said to the newspapers. It was about what she intended to say and, when she had started to put on her hat and coat in the Green Cottage writing-room, about what she intended to reveal.

For all his statesmanship and his undoubted achievements, Mond had been at the centre of more controversy than most men attract in a lifetime. Much of the malevolance against him, especially during the war, was understandable, if hardly justified, but not the venom and the accusations that continued long after the Armistice when there were many who wished to see him publicly discredited. Years later, one such individual was Ethel Brunner, though her motive was certainly not inspired by some ill-defined patriotism.

It mattered not to her whether Mond had led an extraordinary double life during the war, not in the strict sense of a Philby or Blunt of modern times, but as someone with sympathies towards his ancestral homeland, an invaluable gatherer of information to which, as a Privy Counsellor and Minister, he would have had both opportunity and access. Then there had been the explosion at the Silvertown Works and the share dealings of the Mond Nickel Company which preceded a demand for him to be tried as a traitor. Away from the war, what was the truth behind Brunner Mond's almost unbelievable good fortune in acquiring, at a knockdown price, the Billingham Ammonia and Nitrates Plant, with its rich bed of anhydrite?

Ethel Brunner was certainly hinting to the press that she knew a great deal about the Billingham transaction which had occurred whilst Mond was a serving member of the Cabinet, and more than anything, this was probably the crux of what she intended to reveal... and it would have mortified Roscoe Brunner.

*****

So, if one turns the case on its head and views the whole sorry sequel from a different perspective, what could have happened in the Green Cottage writing-room on the evening of Wednesday, November 3rd, 1926? Why did Roscoe Brunner carry his revolver to a fateful rendezvous with his wife and what became of the documents Ethel Brunner may have been about to use against Sir Alfred Mond?

The Lord Reading announcement had unquestionably been the final, excruciating blow. Roscoe Brunner, unaware of what was going on between Mond and Reading, had returned to London, from the Conservative Association dinner, in Cheshire, fully expecting confirmation of his own appoint-

The Marquess of Reading (Rufus Isaacs) when Lord Chief Justice.

ment onto the I.C.I. board. He normally spent his weekends at Cavendish Square, but on this occasion, and obviously anticipating there would at last be something to celebrate, he joined his wife at Green Cottage to await the call from Mond. He was still at Green Cottage on the Monday and he did not return to Cavendish Square until the Tuesday morning, by which time he must have been fully aware that, once again, he had become the victim of Mond's unmerciful litany and deceit.

His ambitions had foundered on the rocks of the Aquitania Agreement and though he may have been resigned to the inevitable, it is not difficult to imagine his wife's outrage, nor her desire for vengeance. When they parted that morning, Brunner may have suspected that the consequences might be dire for, as the psychiatrist Haydn Brown had told the police: 'Of late, Mr Brunner had no power to persuade her on any point whatsoever. His expostulations only aroused her determination to be energetic all the more.'

In any event, it seems that some time during Tuesday, Roscoe Brunner contacted Alfred Robinson, at Belmont Hall, and instructed him to send the revolver to London, though even at this stage we cannot be sure whether he planned suicide or murder. What we can deduce is that something must have occurred to exacerbrate the situation after Brunner had returned to London from his trip to Northwich, where he would have had ample opportunity to have personally acquired the revolver from Belmont Hall. That 'something' could only have been the Lord Reading announcement!

Certainly, on the Tuesday evening, and whilst his wife was commencing her round of calls on the newspapers, Brunner dined alone in the Cavendish Square boardroom, attended by the steward, William Beldan. He retired to bed at ten o'clock and the next morning was served tea in bed. Beldan stated that Brunner seemed in his usual spirits, a view endorsed by the Brunner Mond office staff who said that he had talked to them throughout the morning in his customary, cheerful manner. In mid-afternoon he strolled down to the Bath Club to enjoy a few hours of conviviality and a rubber of whist and, maybe, he was hoping against all hope that his wife would not take the I.C.I.

directorship snub too far.

At about four o'clock Ethel arrived at the Bath Club and though they were engaged in only a brief conversation, Brunner's demeanour changed noticeably, so that when he later emerged into Dover Street, he seemed uncharacteristically ill at ease, as noticed by the doorman of the Bath Club.

Satisfied that she had alerted the press, Ethel Brunner's intention was probably to make one last stab at persuading her husband to personally carry the fight to the shareholders of Brunner Mond & Company. His passiveness had been bad enough over his removal from the chairmanship, but now, and with some justification, there was no longer anything to lose.

However, loyalty comes in many forms; loyalty to one's family, country and sovereign and Roscoe Brunner was unswerving in all of them, but above all he was loyal to his father's great legacy and for all his personal disappointment, he would have been unable to stomach the thought of a scandal, even by implication, engulfing Brunner Mond & Company.

At Green Cottage and with the domestic niceties over, the conversation must have turned to the I.C.I. situation and the fact that Ethel had been speaking with journalists. Yet it is scarcely believable that this alone could have provoked Roscoe Brunner to seriously contemplate murder and what seems to have changed the atmosphere was his wife's revelation that she was threatening to return to the newspapers.

Unable to stop her, as Haydn Brown had said, Brunner may have decided there and then to return to his apartment and take his own life. Unfortunately, the chauffeur had not arrived with the car and Brunner was, therefore, forced to return to the writing-room where he was surely confronted with his wife also preparing to leave the house. There had not been any telephone calls and no hastily arranged social visits, but she too was planning to accompany him on his return into the city and, without a pre-arranged appointment, it seems obvious that her only possible destination must have been the self-same newspaper offices where, at precisely the same late hour on the previous evening, she had been courteously received. The difference this time was that she intended to give the journalists conclusive proof, i.e. documents with which to positively incriminate Mond in a fearful scandal.

It was this threat, and this alone, that, if he was responsible for his wife's death, turned Roscoe Brunner from a broken man contemplating suicide into a cold-blooded killer.

Standing by the writing-desk, Ethel would have been putting on her hat and coat when he walked behind her and, with a single bullet, shot her through the neck. His final act would then have been to kneel down beside his wife's body and shoot himself. There had not been a quarrel, no raised voices and nothing to alert members of staff elsewhere in the house and, as the chairman of the council in his home town of Northwich put it, '...Mr Roscoe Brunner died a martyr to duty'.

This, based upon a re-examination of the available evidence, ties up many of the loose ends, but not all of them. Critically, it does not explain the final position of the bodies, nor how the drawer came to be opened above them, a 'virtual impossibility', said Dr Nobbs, the police surgeon. The drawer, of course, could have been opened by Holdstock or Dorrington during the 'missing minutes' when Mrs Attwell went off to find a policeman, but given the circumstances, one has to conclude that this seems extremely unlikely and, in any event, the open drawer was entirely consistent with the general untidiness of the writing-room.

In a further example of the ham-fisted way in which the police tackled the case, the housekeeper was never asked if she had noticed, when she made her grim discovery, whether papers and documents were scattered about the room, or if the drawer was open above the bodies.

There are three other possible causes of death to be considered, though none were examined at the inquest, or by the investigating officers. Firstly, the revolver may have gone off accidentally during a struggle. Secondly, Roscoe and Ethel Brunner agreed to a suicide pact. Neither seem particularly plausible. A struggle suggests raised voices and a violent argument, whilst a suicide pact is inevitably accompanied by a suicide note, though Holdstock did claim in his statement that Mrs Brunner had once said to him, some years earlier, that if she ever went down in the world, she would do away with herself and her family!

The third explanation, admittedly rather melodramatic but nevertheless feasible, especially in the light of happenings that were to occur at Green Cottage in the aftermath of the tragedy, is that an undetected assailant, or assailants, shot them both, with Brunner's revolver, ransacked the writing-room and then slipped away into the night, leaving the scene to appear one of murder and suicide.

The maid, Bella Scott, remembered hearing the door-bell ring and when she went out into the hall she saw Brunner alighting the dimly-lit stairs, but who can say that he was definitely alone? Dr Nobbs was adamant, of course, that Brunner had fired both shots and yet, surely, the issue here was why seasoned detectives failed to call upon forensic evidence to emphatically rule out the existence of a third person, or persons. Since the turn of the century new methods of forensic analysis were turning crime detection into a science through finger-printing, blood groups and ballistics. If nothing else, finger-printing might have resolved who opened the drawer above the bodies and who, if not the Brunners themselves, was responsible for the disarray in the writing-room.

It was a tantalising twist and there was to be an incredible post-script.

CHAPTER EIGHTEEN
GREEN COTTAGE SENSATION

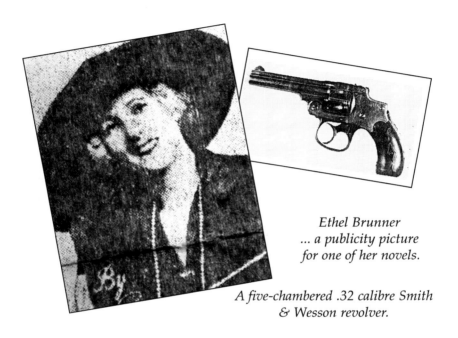

*Ethel Brunner
... a publicity picture
for one of her novels.*

*A five-chambered .32 calibre Smith
& Wesson revolver.*

The Brunner case was riddled with ambiguities and uncertainties throughout, but this was never more evident than on the evening of Roscoe and Ethel Brunner's funerals, just six days after the tragic couple had met their untimely end. Shortly before eight o'clock, on Tuesday, November 9th, and with the last remnants of the domestic staff visiting a local public house, Green Cottage was sensationally broken into, apparently by two men aware that the property was temporarily unattended. But what made this crime so remarkable was that the intruders, burglars to the police, ignored valuable items of silverware, trampled underfoot expensive jewellery and cast aside various small amounts of cash. Indeed, as far as it could be ascertained, not a single item was taken. These were no ordinary 'burglars' and the police, again headed by Det. Insp. Albert Eve, were baffled by the lack of motive. All they had to go on was an eye-witness account from a neighbour who observed 'two well-dressed gentlemen in dark overcoats' leaving Green Cottage at about 9.30pm and then driving away in a motor-car. The police were also able to ascertain that the intruders had gained access to Green Cottage by way of a drawing-room window and they had left behind a trail of muddy footprints.

This time, and with considerably more diligence than they had displayed in their original investigation, the police called upon forensics to take footprint casts and fingerprints. It did not help and what the News of the World termed 'an amazing and lamentable outrage' passed into police statistics as another unsolved crime. Yet what was astonishing about the break-in was that the trail of muddy footprints led directly to the Green Cottage writing-room and, precisely as on the previous Wednesday when they had been called to commence their murder inquiries, the police discovered it in the same state of disarray. Just as before, the room had been been ransacked and the writing-desk had again warranted the most attention. Bills, cheque books, correspondence and documents had all been examined and flung aside, and the inference was clear.

On this occasion, the Brunners themselves could certainly not have been responsible and whoever the culprits were, they were not interested in trinkets and baubels... only Ethel Brunner's private papers!

Predictably, Det, Insp. Eve, a master sleuth of mind-boggling incompetence, dismissed the latest incident as a mere coincidence. He was of the steadfast opinion that it had been the work of what he termed 'ghoulish opportunists' who had probably been seeking documents connected with Spahlinger's cure for turbucolosis, a theory subsequently discounted by the doctor himself.

What efforts the police went to in order to check out the fingerprints and footprints we cannot say; the file appertaining to the break-in would seem to have have long since been destroyed and there is no reference whatsoever to the matter in the Brunner case notes. Indeed, there is absolutely nothing to suggest that anyone was ever questioned, let alone apprehended, and little correalation was made with the Brunner deaths.

Yet, in the context of this narrative and taking into account the entire evidence, the break-in at Green Cottage, audacious and extraordinary in the extreme, lends overwhelming weight to the contention that there was something far more sinister about the Brunner deaths than the police ever appreciated.

Whatever their purpose, these were men on a desperate mission and, that being so, is it so far-fetched to believe that they were attempting to locate the self-same documents which may have been at the root of the murder, or murders?

We must return, as ever, to Sir Alfred Mond and the all-pervading odour of I.C.I. merger. No-one could ever point the finger directly at Mond, or even suggest that he would personally resort to common burglary, but he was rich and powerful and, as the saying goes, 'absence of evidence is not always evidence of absence'.

We can be sure that if Ethel Brunner, a veritable loose cannon, did intend to expose Mond, then he certainly would have known what she was up to. There had been her remonstrations on the doorstep of his home in Lowndes Square, his unconventional approach to the coroner and then his letter to Brigadier General Sir William Horwood, the Commissioner of the Metropolitan Police. When he visited the coroner, was he genuinely assisting with inquiries, or was he attempting to determine whether anything incriminating had been found amongst Ethel Brunner's papers? And, since the police had taken away a considerable number of personal papers during their investigation, could the letter to Horwood have been written from a sense of relief that a potentially mortifying blow to the I.C.I. merger had not surfaced?

What may be construed is that if Mond, who at this time was trying to wring a viscountancy out of the Prime Minister, Stanley Baldwin, apparently 'to project his international responsibilities in the business world', was in any way implicated in the break-in, he must have spent an agonising six days worrying about the ramifications of the 'missing' documents.

The Brunners' daughter, Princess Shelagh had been expected to return on the day following the funerals and, in the family circle, it was anticipated she would immediately commence closing down the property. That Tuesday evening had therefore presented the one window of opportunity to instigate a thorough search of Ethel Brunner's private papers. It was the first time that Green Cottage had not, literally, been crawling with police and, furthermore, the authorities, never anxious to delve too deeply into the Brunner deaths, would have been reluctant to reopen the case which, to all intent and purpose, had been properly concluded through the inquest proceedings.

So who were these two well-dressed men who seemed to know their way around Green Cottage? A distinct possibility must, again, be Holdstock and Dorrington, the chauffeur and butler, who, according to the maid, Bella Scott, did not appear at the pub with the others until late in the evening. There was also servant-talk afterwards that they were responsible for the break-in, possibly to recover IOUs which Ethel Brunner was in the habit of demanding when she occasionally advanced them cash in advance of their wages.

Said Bella Scott: 'Holdstock and Dorrington were as thick as thieves - you never knew quite what they were up to and the others thought they broke in so they wouldn't have to pay money back when Shelagh returned.'

This may appear credible, but why go to such ends simply for the sake of an IOU? Besides, if a significant amount of money had been involved, then surely the suspicions of even the most incompetent detective would have been aroused. And, of course, if Holdstock and Dorrington were in such pecuniary straits as to stage a daring raid for the purpose of recovering their IOUs, would they not, in the process, have seized the chance to pocket one or two valuable items?

Whoever the intruders were, there is no discernible, or logical, reason for the break-in, other than it was carried out to steal documents from Ethel Brunner's personal effects; documents which would then, no doubt, have been delivered to their paymaster. Yet, as one final, remarkable incident in the saga was to emphatically reveal, they left empty-handed.

Four months later, in the early hours of Saturday, March 19, 1927, detectives from Scotland Yard were again called to Green Cottage. Princess Shelagh and her husband had forsaken the house but, as probate had only been granted that very week on Roscoe and Ethel Brunner's wills, they had not commenced removing internal effects. A caretaker, making his nightly rounds, discovered that the back-door to Green Cottage had been forced and, incredibly, there had been another frantic search through Ethel Brunner's private papers. And, just as before, the intruders had ignored jewellery and valuable artefacts!

Take it as you will, read into it what you like, but there was something else, in my opinion inalienable proof that the Brunner deaths, the break-ins at Green Cottage and the race to force through the I.C.I. merger were enmeshed in a web of deceit about which the inquest jury, the press and the public knew nothing.

Saturday, March 19, 1927, the day of the second break-in at Green Cottage, was also, astonishingly, the day of Imperial Chemical Industries' first annual meeting!

This took place at Winchester House, London and Sir Alfred Mond, presiding, inadvertently gave the strongest possible hint as to what had been going on in those tragic days of the previous November.

Said Mond: 'When we started the merger the directors of the various merging companies which form the fusion could not, of course, of themselves form a definite, or conclusive, opinion as to how far their shareholders would accept the invitation to exchange the shares in their respective companies for shares in Imperial Chemical Industries. We had to take a certain amount of risk on this, but those of us chiefly responsible were quite certain that we should get a response of such a nature and of such a character as would at any rate pass the controlling interest in the old companies to the new company, and justify us in taking the risk...'

Ethel Brunner was one individual with a powerful voice who was prepared to use every means at her disposal to challenge the merger proposals. She might have succeeded, and British industrial history may have been rewritten had it not been for the unswerving loyalty of Roscoe Brunner, a depressed and broken man, who had probably utilised the most suitable and convenient repository to dispose of her scandal-threatening documents... the writing-room fire!

The trouble was that those who stood to lose the most could not be sure. Or was it, as the police maintained, all a series of coincidences; that the first break-in just happened to occur on the night before Princess Shelagh's return, that the second break-in followed at the very last moment when Green Cottage was to be finally abandoned, or that it took place on the very day of I.C.I.'s first annual meeting?

At least one thing is certain - the immediate Brunner family maintained their own closely-guarded opinions.

Some years ago, the distinguished science-fiction writer, John Brunner, the grandson of Roscoe and Ethel Brunner, was invited to address a local arts' society in Cheshire. He turned his visit into a mini-pilgrimage to view for himself what was left of the Brunner Mond industrial legacy, but whether he was disappointed or not remains a matter of conjecture for some months later he died, just short of his sixty-first birthday. By nature, John Brunner seldom looked back; his roots and his ancestry held little appeal, although he did agree to be interviewed.

John Brunner's father was Anthony, the eldest son of Roscoe and Ethel. Known as 'Tony' within the family, he apparently suffered serious financial losses in the Wall Street crash and was later badly injured in an accident whilst playing polo. There was also Tony's younger brother, Patrick whose own daughter, April, was a god-daughter of Queen Mary. Then, of course, there was Princess Shelagh, 'Aunt Shelagh'.

'When Aunt Shelagh married the Prince it was a morganic marriage in Liechtenstein,' said John Brunner. 'The Prince was definitely a play-boy and even on the night of their wedding, at Claridge's, he left her to flirt with an actress. It was a loveless marriage and they soon divorced. Aunt Shelagh was eventually remarried, to an Austrian/Hungarian citizen who came to be interred on the Isle of Man during the Second World War.'

Roscoe and Ethel Brunner died years before John Brunner was born, but his grandmother, Ethel, had always been regarded in the family, he said, as a forceful character. 'She was once mistaken for the Queen of Romania and that certainly amused her...'

Regrettably, John Brunner claimed to know little of the events surrounding the actual tragedy. 'I was told only the briefest of details by my father. It was a family scandal not really to be discussed,' he said. 'There may have been something with Sir Alfred Mond, but all I know of him was that it was said that from his death bed, his father, Ludwig Mond, cursed him. The Brunner and Mond families had been close at the time of Ludwig Mond and my great-grandfather, but they grew seriously apart in the next generation.'

Curiously, considering John Brunner was only furnished with the 'briefest of details' about his grandparents' deaths, he had been told of the burglary at Green Cottage on the night of the funerals, but knew nothing of the second break-in, nor the significance of the date coinciding with I.C.I.'s first annual meeting.

'Yes, I have heard the story about the break-in on the night of the funerals. It was said they were looking for a second will which my grandfather may have written.'

This offered a new slant on the mystery, although upon reflection it seems totally implausible, for if Roscoe Brunner had indeed prepared a new will, which is unlikely, he would hardly have kept the document at Green Cottage and, in any event, who from outside the family would have been interested? For the record, probate was granted on wills drawn up by Roscoe and Ethel Brunner and retained by the Cheshire solicitors James H.Wadsworth. Ethel Brunner's will is dated November 28, 1924 and Roscoe Brunner's on January 30th, 1925, the latter presumably to accommodate their daughter Shelagh's marriage to the Prince of Liechtenstein. Furthermore, as Roscoe's brother, Jack, was a named trustee, it is impossible to believe that a second will would have remained undiscovered during the search of personal effects immediately following the deaths.

John Brunner was unable to add anything further but, in correspondence, his sister, Verena Thornton, was rather more forthcoming. The deaths, she said, were a taboo subject in her parents' household, emphatically not to be discussed outside of the family, an edict which remained as late as 1970 and extended to the author W.J.Reader when researching his book into the history of I.C.I..

Verena Thornton recalled: 'Dr Reader contacted my mother for information about the tragedy, but when my Aunt Elaine (Patrick Brunner's widow) heard about it, she put her foot down. It seems that at such a late date there are (or were) people around who felt the the matter was too sensitive for publication.'

Only on two or three other occasions had Verena Thornton ever heard the matter discussed in detail and one theory centred on the premise that Roscoe Brunner had accidentally shot his wife whilst attempting to commit suicide.

She added: 'The only information I have about the tragedy came from my mother, but her interest was not in the event itself, rather in the effect it had on my father. What my mother did tell me, was that there was some story about my grandfather covering up for someone within the company, someone who had been involved in underhand dealings...'

And there the Brunner case must rest, for this is probably as far as we can ever go to solve the mystery, except to say that no empire is ever built without casualties. In the final analysis, it does not matter now who really did the deed; it only matters who willed it and welcomed it when it was done, for murder by subterfuge is no less murder than a gun fired at point-blank range!

CAST OF CHARACTERS

JOHN TOMLINSON BRUNNER - 1st Bart. (created 1895). Born 1842. Co-founder (1873) of Brunner Mond & Co. Served as Member of Parliament for Northwich, Cheshire, 1885-6 and 1887-1910. Privy Counsellor 1906. Died July 1st, 1919.

LUDWIG MOND - Born Cassel, Germany, 1839. Co-founder (1873) Brunner Mond & Co. Formed Mond Nickel Co. with mines in Canada and works near Swansea, 1888. FRS 1891. Died 1909.

ROSCOE BRUNNER - Born 1871. Third son of Sir John Tomlinson Brunner. Director Brunner Mond & Co., 1901-1926. Chairman Brunner Mond & Co 1918 - 1925. Died November 3rd, 1926.

ETHEL BRUNNER - Born 1877. Eldest daughter of Arthur Houston KC. Married Roscoe Brunner 1898. Fiction author. Died November 3rd, 1926.

ALFRED MOND - Born 1868. Liberal Member of Parliament, Chester (1906-1910); Swansea (1910-23); Carmarthen (1924-28). President of Empire Economic Union; President of the World Power Conference, 1928, Chairman of Imperial Chemical Industries 1926 until his death. Championed the cause of Zionism, purchased land in Palestine and pressed for the free state of Israel; Chairman of Economic Board for Palestine. Created 1st Baron Melchett of Landford, in June 1928. The addition of an extra 't' to the name of his home, Melchet Court, was apparently a whim, and in his coat of arms he included crescent moons, in acknowledgment of the family name. Died December 27th, 1930, leaving an estate valued in excess of £1 million. The funeral rites were conducted at Finchley, on December 30th, and I.C.I. factories throughout the world ceased work whilst he was laid to rest. The following day a memorial service was attended in London by over 1,000 employees, colleagues, friends and family. Not a single Brunner name was recorded in the list of mourners.

VIOLET MOND - Lady Melchett. A pioneer in welfare work in Wales; Chairman of the Chelsea Health Society; Freeman of the Borough of Chelsea, created a Dame of the British Empire in 1920. Died September 25th, 1945.

HENRY MOND - 2nd Baron Melchett of Landford. Born 1898. Director of Brunner Mond & Co.; Liberal MP Isle of Ely 1923-24; Conservative MP East Toxteth, Liverpool 1929-30; Deputy Chairman of Imperial Chemical Industries 1940-47. Died January 22nd, 1949. His son, Julian Edward Alfred Mond, 3rd Baron Melchett of Landford, became Chairman of the British Steel Corporation from 1967.

JOHN FOWLER LEECE BRUNNER - 2nd Bart.. Born 1865, eldest son of Sir John Tomlinson Brunner. MP, Leigh Division (Lancashire) 1906-10; Northwich 1910-18; Southport 1923-24. One of the thirteen original Directors of Imperial Chemical Industries. Resigned from the Board in August 1927, bringing two generations of collaboration between the Brunners and Monds to a close. Died January 16th, 1929.

PRINCE FERDINAND ANDREAS JOSEPH MARIA, OF THE HOUSE OF LIECHTENSTEIN - Born Salzburg Jan 18th, 1901. Married Shelagh Salome Brunner, January 14th, 1925. Dissolved by divorce 1934, ecclesiastically annulled 1939. Issue: Christopher von Rietberg, Ethel Elisabeth Olga Mary, Countess von Rietberg, born, 1928, Soos Castle, Melk, Austria. Married secondly (morganic marriage) at Stockholm, September 7th, 1940, Brita, daughter of General Bengt Nordenskiold, Swedish Airforce. Issue: Johannes, Eduard Bengt Henrik Andreas Maria, Count von Rietberg.

SHELAGH SALOME HOUSTON BRUNNER - Daughter of Roscoe & Ethel Brunner. Married Prince Ferdinand Andreas Joseph Maria, of The House of Liechtenstein, January 14th, 1925 (morganic marriage). Dissolved by divorce 1934, ecclesiastically annulled 1939. Married Georg Otto Suppanic. Died November 6th, 1983.

CHRISTOPHER von RIETBERG - Born May 8th, 1926, Green Cottage, Roehampton. Son of Prince Ferdinand Andreas Joseph Maria Liechtenstein and Shelagh Salome Houston Brunner. Served with 15/19 Hussars. Married, May 17th, 1955, Kathleen Hamilton, daughter of Alfred Thayer Mahan, Orangeburg, New York, USA.

RUFUS DANIEL ISAACS - 1st Marquess of Reading (created 1926) - Born London 1860. MP Reading 1904-13; Solicitor General 1910; Attorney General 1910-13; Lord Chief Justice of England 1913-21; High Commissioner and Special Ambassador to USA 1918; Viceroy and Governor General of India, 1921-26; One of the original thirteen Directors of Imperial Chemical Industries. Became President of Imperial Chemical Industries. Secretary of State for Foreign Affairs, National Government 1931; Lord Warden of the Cinque Ports, 1934. Died December, 30th, 1935. Son, Gerald Rufus Isaacs, Viscount Earleigh, married Sir Alfred Mond's daughter, Eva.

HARRY DUNCAN McGOWAN - Baron McGowan. Born 1874. Joined Nobel's Explosives Co., 1889; Chairman and Managing Director, Nobel Industries Ltd 1918-1926; KBE 1918; President I.C.I. 1926-30, Chairman and Managing Director 1930 - 1937, Chairman 1937-1950. Died 1961.

JOHN FLETCHER MOULTON - Baron Moulton. Born 1844. Barrister Middle Temple 1874; QC 1885; Judge, Court of Appeal, 1906-12. Minister of Munitions 1915-1919. Liberal MP Clapham, South Hackney, Launceston. Chairman British Dyestuffs Corporation 1919-21. Died March 9th, 1921.

SIR EDWARD CARSON - Baron Carson of Duncairn (created 1921). Solicitor General Ireland, 1892; Solicitor General 1900-1906; Attorney General 1915; First Lord of the Admirality 1917; Member of the War Cabinet without Portfolio 1917-18; Lord of Appeal 1921-29. Died October 22nd, 1933.

WILLIAM HESKETH LEVER - 1st Viscount Leverhulme of the Western Isles (created 1922) . Born 1851. Chairman Lever Brothers Ltd and founder of Port Sunlight. Liberal MP Wirral Division (Cheshire) 1906-10. Created Baronet 1911, Baron 1917. Died May, 1925.

SAMUEL INGLEBY ODDIE - Born 1869. Studied medicine Edinburgh University, later joining Naval Medical Service. General practitioner New Malden. Studied for the Bar; Barrister Middle Temple 1901; Coroner for Westminster and South West London 1902. Notable cases: 'Charing Cross trunk murder', 1928; RO 1 airship disaster, 1932. Retired 1939 when it was said that his combination of wide practical experience, both of law and medicine, had made him an excellent coroner. Died May, 1945.

DET. INSP. ALBERT EVE - Born Bishopsgate, London 1881. Joined Metropolitan Police 1902, rising through ranks to Divisional Det. Insp. Completed 27 years' service. Retired with 'excellent record', Wandsworth Division, June 1929.

IMPERIAL CHEMICAL INDUSTRIES (I.C.I.)

On its formation, in December 1926, Imperial Chemical Industries had 33,000 employees and listed amongst its products, chemicals, explosives and accessories, fetilisers, insecticides, dyestuffs, domestic chemicals, leathercloth, printing, sporting ammunition and paints. Seventy years later, I.C.I. had 725 million issued shares and almost 250,000 shareholders. It had 64,000 employees worldwide, more than 8,000 products and manufacturing sites at over 200 locations in more than thirty countries. In 1993, the company began to formally demerge. In 1995, I.C.I.'s annual turnover was £10,269 million with a pre-tax profit of £951 million.

BIBLIOGRAPHY & REFERENCES

The Brunner Papers - Sidney Jones Library, University of Liverpool
Parliamentary Debates (Hansard)
The First Fifty Years of Brunner Mond & Company
The Mond Legacy, Jean Goodman
A History of the Alkali Division, A.S.Irvine
I.C.I. The Company That Changed Our Lives, Carol Kennedy
A Hundred Years of Alkali in Cheshire, W.F.L.Dick
The Life of Ludwig Mond, J.M.Cohen
The Chemical Industry's Participation in
Industrial Relations, J.K.Bottomley
A History of Winnington Hall, A.S.Irvine
Imperial Chemical Industries: A History, W.J.Reader
Sir John Brunner, Radical Plutocrat, 1842-1919, Stephen E.Koss
The History of Unilever, Charles Wilson
Alfred Mond, The First Lord Melchett, Hector Bolitho
White Mischief, James Fox
Memoirs of a London County Coroner, H.R.Oswald
Notable British Trials, edited Geoffrey Clarke
Celia and Her Friends, Ethel Brunner,
The Donwfall of the Liberal Party 1914-1935, Trevor Wilson
I Bought a Newspaper, Claude Morris
Rufus Isaacs, First Marquess of Reading, Marquess of Reading
Lloyd George - The Goat in the Wilderness, Jonathan Cape
War Memories, David Lloyd George
Tempestuous Journey - Lloyd George: His Life and Times, Frank Owen

REFERENCES
The British Newspaper Library, London
Cheshire County Record Office
Chester City Library
Greater London Record Office
General Register Office
Battersea Library
A wide range of newspapers and journals has been consulted, of which the most important include: The Times, Daily Herald, Daily Telegraph, London Evening Standard, Daily Express, Daily Mail, Morning Post, New Witness, Sunday Express, Sunday Pictorial, Sunday Chronicle, News of the World, Weekly Dispatch, Manchester Guardian, Warrington Guardian, Northwich Guardian, Chester Chronicle, Northwich Chronicle, Cheshire Life, Westminster Gazette, ICI Alkali News.